What We Cook on Cape Cod

Marula

An imprint of Arcadia Publishing

What We Cook on Cape Cod
by The Village Improvement Society
Barnstable, Massachusetts

A Marula Historical Reprint
Originally published in 1911

Published by Arcadia Publishing
Charleston SC

ISBN 978-0-7385-9493-4

Printed in the United States of America

For all general information contact Arcadia Publishing at:
Telephone 843-853-2070
Fax 843-853-0044
E-mail sales@arcadiapublishing.com
For customer service and orders:
Toll-Free 1-888-313-2665

Visit us on the Internet at www.arcadiapublishing.com

WHAT WE COOK ON CAPE COOD

FOREWORD BY

JOSEPH C. LINCOLN

PUBLISHED BY THE

VILLAGE IMPROVEMENT SOCIETY

BARNSTABLE, MASS.

Printed by F. B. & F. P. Goss, Hyannis, Mass.

Foreword

A Cape Cod cook book! you who stray
Far from the old sand-bordered Bay,
The cranberry bogs, the tossing pines,
The wind-swept beaches frothing lines,
You city dwellers who, like me,
Were children, playing by the sea,
Whose fathers manned the vanished ships—
Hark! do I hear you smack your lips?

A Cape Cod cook book! My oh my!
I know that twinkle on your eye,
And why you're pricking up your ears,
You've turned the clock back thirty years.
I know that smile of yours; it tells
Of chowder, luscious as it smells;
And when you laugh aloud, you dream
Of berry dumpling, bathed in cream.

A Cape Cod cook book! Why, I'll bet
The doughnut crock could tempt you yet!
Those Cape Cod doughnuts! Yes you'll take
A few of those, and then some cake—
The frosted kinds—and—let me see—
Some pie, of course, and—Mercy me!
You can't go on; it wouldn't do!
One takes on weight at forty-two.

A Cape Cod cook book! Here they are!
A breath from every cookie jar,
A whiff from ovens spicy sweet,
Two hundred secrets—good to eat!
Thanksgiving, clambake, picnic grove,
Each lends a taste, a treasure trove;
And here they are for you to buy—
What's that? You've bought one? So have I.

JOSEPH C. LINCOLN.

Harwichport, Mass., August, 1911.

Index

Bread

Polly's Nut Bread.—Two cups of graham and one cup of white flour, one-quarter cup of sugar, one teaspoonful of soda and one-half teaspoonful of salt. Sift together and add any bran that may remain in the sifter. Add one-half cup of molasses, one and one-half cups of sour milk and one cup of walnut meats. Bake in bread pan three-quarters of an hour.—[* * * *

Maple Sugar Biscuit.—One pint of flour, two rounding teaspoonfuls of baking powder, one-quarter teaspoonful of salt. Sift together and add one rounding tablespoonful of butter worked into the flour, add one-half cup of maple sugar broken in pieces the size of a pea. Add a half cup of milk and enough more to make a dough a little stiffer than for biscuits. Work on the bread board till well mixed. Roll and cut with small biscuit cutter. Bake in a quick oven. If made and baked right this will be like baking powder biscuit with brown spots of melted sugar through them.—[Mrs. E. A. Handy.

Virginia Batter Bread.—One quart of milk brought to the boiling point, one pint of corn meal, butter the size of an egg, one teaspoonful of salt. Cook and stir like mush. When cold add six eggs well beaten, one pint of cream or buttermilk in which a teaspoonful of soda has been dissolved. Put in a baking dish and cover till it rises. Bake.—[Mrs. J. D. Livingston.

Improved Popovers.—Two eggs beaten very light, one and one-half cups milk, one and one-half cups pastry flour, one-half teaspoonful salt. Beat together with an egg beater five minutes. Grease the cups and set on the stove to heat. Drop a piece of butter the size of a pea in each cup and let it melt. This gives a crisp crust to the popover. Bake in stone cups half an hour or until they are firm and will not fall when taken out.—[Mrs. E. A. Handy.

Whole Wheat Bread.—Three cups of whole wheat flour, three teaspoonfuls of baking powder, one-half teaspoonful of salt, two teaspoonfuls of sugar, milk. Sift together thoroughly the flour, baking powder, salt and sugar, add enough milk to make a dough just stiff enough to handle conveniently. Shape into a loaf and place in a deep, buttered pan, handling as little as possible. Allow it to stand five minutes before putting in the oven. Bake slowly and for a longer time than for white bread. Protect the loaf with a piece of buttered paper, putting the buttered side next the bread.—[Mrs. H. M. Hutchings.

Brown Bread.—Three cups of rye meal, three cups of corn meal, one pint of molasses, one quart of sour milk, half cream if possible, one teaspoonful of soda, salt. Steam five hours.—[Mrs. Vaughan Bacon.

Sally Lunn, for Tea.—Three eggs well beaten, one cup of warm milk, two tablespoonfuls of butter, two tablespoonfuls of sugar, one-half an yeast cake, three cups of flour. Set to rise about twelve o'clock and an hour before supper put in muffin pans to rise again for half an hour, then bake.—[Mrs. George Hussey.

ON CAPE COD

Oat Meal Bread.—Pour one quart of boiling water over one pint of Quaker Rolled Oats. When luke warm add one small cup of molasses, one-half of a yeast cake dissolved in one cup of water, one teaspoonful of salt, two quarts of flour sifted or cut in. Let rise over night. Do not stir or knead in the morning. Let it rise a short time in pans before baking. This makes one dozen muffins or two loaves.—[Mrs. Ruth E. Chipman.

*Togus Bread.—Two cups of Indian meal, one cup of flour, two cups of sweet milk, one cup of sour milk, one-half cup of molasses, salt, one tablespoonful of soda. Boil four hours. Put in the oven if you like.—[Mrs. J. M. Day.

*Scotch Bread.—One pound of flour, scant half cup of sugar, half a pound of butter. Mix butter and sugar, then add the flour; mix without liquid until it is a smooth paste. Roll out, not too thin; nip round the edges.—[E. L. F.

Something New in Corn Bread.—One and one-quarter cups flour, three-quarters cup corn meal, two teaspoonfuls baking powder, one-half teaspoonful salt. Sift together and work in two tablespoons butter. Add one well beaten egg and one-half cup milk. Beat all together and drop in spoonfuls on buttered tin. Bake in moderate oven.—[Mrs. E. A. Handy.

Brown Bread.—Two cups of graham flour, one cup of corn meal, one cup of molasses, one teaspoon of soda, dissolved in the milk, one teaspoonful of salt, one cup of sour milk, one cup of sweet milk. Steam four hours.—[Mrs. F. H. Thayer.

*From Midsummer Cook Book.

Breakfast Gems.—One cup of milk, one cup of water, one well beaten egg, one tablespoonful of melted butter, one tablespoonful of baking powder sifted with two cups of flour. Mix in the order given and pour into iron gem pans heated hot, first putting a piece of butter in each partition. Bake quickly in a very hot oven.—[Mrs. F. B. Goss.

Water Gems.—Two cups of water, add one cup of milk, two and one-half cups of flour, beat about five minutes. Bake in very hot gem pans very freely buttered. Bake thirty-five minutes.—[Mrs. Davis.

German Apple Cake.—One and one-half tablespoonfuls of butter and two and one-half tablespoonfuls of sugar beaten to a cream. Three cups of flour sifted with two teaspoonfuls of baking powder, add to butter and sugar. Add to this three well beaten eggs and enough rich milk to make a dough stiff enough to handle. Roll dough to fit pans. Slice apples very thin and lay them on the dough plentifully; sprinkle with a little cinnamon and sugar. Bake in a medium oven.—[Mrs. M. A. Timken.

Cream Biscuit.—One quart of flour, four teaspoonfuls of baking powder, one teaspoonful of salt, sift twice, one-quarter cup of thick cream and enough milk to make a stiff dough. Work on the board a few minutes and cut with small round cutter. For picnics try cutting these or any baking powder biscuit the size and shape of half a slice of bread. Bake and when cool split and fill with any sandwich filling. Also try rolling the dough rather thin and spreading one-half with chopped ham, lay the other half on top and cut in squares and bake.—[Mrs. E. A. Handy

ON CAPE COD

PARKER HOUSE ROLLS.—Ingredients: One quart of flour, one yeast cake, one and one-half cups of milk, one-quarter of a cup of sugar, one-quarter of a cup of butter, a very little salt. Put salt and sugar into flour, then add the yeast cake after dissolving in one-quarter of a cup of luke warm water. Heat the milk and add the butter, use when nearly cool. Raise twice, then mould and raise again. Bake in a good oven.—[Mrs. E. D. Crocker.

GERMAN APPLE CAKE.—Make a dough as given for Apple Short Cake. When it is in the pan ready for the oven, cover thick with apples peeled, cored and cut in eighths. Pour over a mixture made of one teaspoonful flour, three teaspoonfuls brown sugar, one-half teaspoonful cinnamon, three tablespoonfuls milk. Bake in hot oven about twenty minutes. Serve hot.—[Mrs. E. A. Handy.

HUCKLEBERRY GRIDDLE CAKES.—One well beaten egg, one pint of milk, one teaspoonful of baking powder, one tablespoonful of sugar, one pint of berries, flour. Bake on a griddle in thin cakes. —[Mrs. George Hussey.

FRUIT ROLLS.—Two cups of flour, one-half cup of lard, one egg, one-half cup of milk and four scant teaspoonfuls of baking powder. Roll out and spread with butter and sugar, one cup of chopped raisins and one-half cup of nuts. Roll up and cut across, then bake.—[Mrs. Job C. Cobb.

DROP BISCUIT.—One cup of cream, one cup of sour milk, one egg, one-half teaspoonful of soda and a little salt, flour for a stiff batter. Drop in spoonfuls on a buttered tin and bake in a quick oven.—[Mrs. Mary Freeman Hinckley.

APPLE SHORT CAKE.—Two cups sifted pastry flour, two teaspoonfuls baking powder, one teaspoonful salt, one tablespoonful butter, one tablespoonful lard, one egg, one-half cup milk. Sift the dry ingredients together and work in the butter and lard. Beat the egg light and add the milk. Mix this with the flour, etc. Work till smooth and roll out to fit a round pan. Bake and split, fill with hot apple sauce. This can be made without the egg but is not nearly as good.—[Mrs. E. A. Handy.

POTATO ROLLS.—Scald one cup of milk with one tablespoonful of butter and one of sugar. When cool add one teaspoonful of salt and one-quarter cake of yeast dissolved in a little water, add flour enough to make a sponge. Let it rise to double its bulk then add two beaten eggs and three small hot boiled potatoes rubbed through a sieve. Add flour enough to make it as stiff as bread dough, let it rise again. Roll out and cut with a biscuit cutter. Let them rise, and bake ten minutes. Very good.—[Mrs. F. H. Thayer.

COFFEE CAKES.—Cream one cup of butter with three cups of sugar, add three well beaten eggs, one cup of milk, three teaspoonfuls of baking powder and flour enough to roll out. Roll half an inch thick, sprinkle with cinnamon and roll up. Cut half an inch across; dip one end in sugar and bake sugar side up.—[* * * *

BROWN BREAD.—One cup of Indian meal, one cup of rye meal, one cup of bread flour, one cup of molasses, two level teaspoonfuls of soda, a little salt, two cups of water. Steam four hours. One cup of raisins may be added.—[Mrs. Leslie Jones.

ON CAPE COD

Corn Bread Omelet.—Sift together three-quarters of a cup of corn meal, one-quarter of a cup of flour, one-half a teaspoon salt, one tablespoon sugar. Beat one egg very light and add one-half a cup of sour milk, one-half a cup of sweet milk and one-fourth teaspoon soda dissolved in a little of the sweet milk. Beat this into the dry mixture and pour into a hot frying pan in which there is a large tablespoon melted butter. Let it heat for a minute on the stove and then pour gently over it one cup of sweet milk. Bake in a moderate oven half an hour. This should be creamy and yet firm enough to cut and serve.—[Mrs. E. A. Handy.

Pone.—Pour one cup of boiling water over one cup of white corn meal, let stand till luke warm. Separate the yolks of three eggs and beat them into the meal one at a time. Stir in one and one-half cups of luke warm milk, a pinch of salt, one small teaspoonful of baking powder and butter the size of an egg. Bake one-half hour.—[Mrs. Davis.

French Rusks. Two cups of scalded milk, one quarter of a cup of butter, one quarter of a cup of sugar, one teaspoonful of salt, one yeast cake dissolved in one-quarter of a cup of warm water and three cups of flour. Make a batter of all the ingredients and let it rise; when risen add an egg and flour enough to knead. Let it rise and shape as rolls. When nearly done brush with vanilla and water and sprinkle with sugar. Bake in a moderate oven.—[Mrs. Leslie Jones.

Crisped Crackers.—Split butter crackers and spread thinly with butter. Put in a pan and brown in the oven. Serve with soup.—[* * * *

Muffins

Fried Rye Muffins.—One and one-half cups rye meal, one and one-half cups white flour, one teaspoonful salt, three teaspoonfuls baking powder, one tablespoonful of sugar. Sift together and add two eggs beaten light and one cup of milk. Drop in spoonfuls in smoking hot fat and fry like doughnuts.—[Mrs. E. A. Handy.

Muffins.—Two cups of flour, four teaspoonfuls of baking powder, half a teaspoonful of salt, one tablespoonful of sugar, sift together. Add one well beaten egg, one cup of milk and two tablespoonfuls of melted butter.—[Miss Annie Gorham Hinckley.

Oatmeal Muffins.—One cup Quaker oats, pour over them one pint boiling water. Let stand three hours, then add one-half cup molasses, one teaspoonful (rounded) salt, one-half yeast cake dissolved in one-half cup warm water, 1 quart bread flour or enough to make a stiff batter. Beat well and rise over night. In the morning beat it hard and fill muffin pans. When it rises to double the size bake. Rub with butter while hot. This is good baked in a loaf.—[Mrs. E. A. Handy.

Soups

Lettuce Soup.—Take a knuckle of veal, and boil gently on the back of the range 5 hours. Set away to cool, and skim off the fat when cold. Take two heads of lettuce, and boil in the stock till it is colored. Thicken with a little flour, add a cup of cream.—[Miss Julia G. Davis.

*Clam Broth with Whipped Cream.—To a quart of clams, add a pint of water, and simmer on the back of the range an hour. Take off and strain. Have bouillon cups filled with hot water five minutes or more before serving. Heat broth, turn water from cups and fill with broth about two-thirds full. Cover with whipped cream.—[Miss Julia G. Davis.

*Lobster Soup.—Put the bones of the lobster on to boil in water enough to cover them. Boil one quart of milk. Fry one slice of onion cut fine in one tablespoonful of butter. When the onion is yellow skim it out and add to the butter two tablespoonfuls of flour. Add gradually the boiling milk. Season highly with salt and pepper. Boil fifteen or twenty minutes. Dry the coral and sift it into the soup. Add enough of the water in which the bones were boiled to make it the proper thickness. Put the fat of the lobster into the tureen. Pour the soup over it. Add one cup of lobster meat cut in small pieces.—[Miss H. L. Day.

*From the Midsummer Cook Book.

WHAT WE COOK

Asparagus Stew.—One quart of good beef stock, add one can of asparagus tips and boil till tender. Add the following meat balls: Take equal quantities of round of beef and fresh pork chopped very fine. Add two or three onions, chopped and fried in butter, a small quantity of soaked bread, five eggs, pepper and salt. Mix well and make into small balls, roll in cracker dust or zwiback. Boil in the soup till tender. Add a little thickening and a little parsley. Serve hot.—[Mrs. M. A. Timken.

St. Gemain Soup.—Put one can of peas (leaving out half a cup) into a stew pan, add one-half an onion, a bit of bay leaf, a sprig of parsley, a bit of mace, half a teaspoonful of sugar, one teaspoonful of salt, one saltspoonful of pepper. Simmer one-half hour, mash and add three cups of stock (or water). Let it come to the boiling point and rub through a sieve. Melt one tablespoonful of butter, add one tablespoonful of cornstarch and pour on slowly the hot stock. Cook ten minutes, add one cup of milk and the remainder of the peas. Heat and serve with croutons. —[Mrs. H. M. Hutchings.

Tomato Soup for Canning.—One peck of ripe tomatoes, washed and cut in pieces. Wet six tablespoonfuls of cornstarch in enough water to make it smooth and add to the tomatoes. Fry four large onions in half a pound of butter until well browned but not burned. Put with the tomatoes and boil until thoroughly cooked, stirring all the time. Add one pound of white sugar, salt and pepper to taste and two quarts of boiling water. Strain through a colander and then through a cheese cloth. Put back on the stove and bring to a boil and can.—[Mrs. Peterson.

CLARET SOUP.—Pour one pint of boiling water into one pint of claret and add a little lemon juice and half a cup of sugar. Moisten one tablespoonful of arrowroot with cold water and add to the hot soup. Put in the double boiler for a few minutes and add a little cooked tapioca before serving.—[Mrs. J. D. Livingston.

BAKED BEAN SOUP.—Boil cold baked beans with a sliced onion and a little water and stewed tomato till soft, press through a sieve, add one tablespoonful of butter rubbed smooth with one tablespoonful of flour and boil up once.—[Mrs. E. A. Handy.

VEGETABLE SOUP WITHOUT STOCK.—One-third cup of carrot, one and one-half cups of potato, one-third cup of turnip, one-half cup of celery, one-half an onion, one quart of water, one-half tablespoonful of finely chopped parsley, five tablespoonfuls of butter, salt and pepper. Wash and scrape carrot, wash and pare potatoes and turnip, cut in dice, peel onion and slice very thin. Prepare the vegetables before measuring. Cook all the vegetables except the potatoes in four tablespoonfuls of butter for ten minutes stirring all the time, add the potatoes and cook two minutes, add the water and boil one hour. Add the remaining butter and the parsley. Season with salt and pepper.—[Mrs. Maurice Hallett.

CHICKEN GUMBO.—Take the necks, backs and wings of three broilers, one quart of okra, six large tomatoes skinned and sliced, one large onion chopped fine, two bell peppers sliced without seeds, two slices of bacon chopped fine. Fry all in butter, putting in the okra last. Put in a soup kettle with two quarts of water and simmer two hours. Add a little cooked rice and serve.—[Mrs. J. D. Livingston.

Potato Soup.—Boil three good-sized potatoes in water. Boil one pint milk. Fry one slice onion, one carrot, one slice turnip, cut fine, in one heaping tablespoonful butter until yellow. Skim out, and add to the potato also one sprig of parsley. Rub the potato through a strainer and add to the milk. Stir one heaping tablespoonful flour into the butter in which the vegetables were cooked and add to the soup, with one teaspoonful salt, one saltspoonful pepper. Strain and serve.—[Miss H. L. Day.

Lobster Soup.—One good-sized or two small lobsters chopped not very fine, three hard crackers pounded very fine. Mix the cracker and tomalley with a piece of butter size of an egg. Add pepper and salt to taste and work all well together. Boil one quart of milk and pour gradually over the paste, stirring well. Then put in the chopped lobster and boil up once, stirring all the time. Grate the coral and add, if you have it.—[Miss H. L. Day.

Black Bean Soup.—Soak one pint of black beans over night, the next morning drain them and boil in two quarts of fresh water. Slice and fry one small onion in a tablespoonful butter, add it to the beans, and celery root if you have it, with one-quarter of a pound of salt pork or a ham bone. Simmer four or five hours until the beans soften. Add cold water often to check boiling, leaving two quarts of water when done. Rub the beans through a colander, boil again and add a pinch of salt, a pinch of red pepper, a saltspoonful of mustard, a scant tablespoonful of flour, and a tablespoonful of butter rubbed together to prevent the beans from settling. Slice two hard boiled eggs and half a lemon thin and place in the tureen, add half a glass of sherry to the soup and pour over eggs and lemon.—[Grace B. Holway.

ON CAPE COD

Lobster Soup.—Put the bones of the lobster on to boil in water enough to cover them. Boil one quart of milk. Fry one onion cut fine in a tablespoonful of butter till yellow, skim out the onion and add to the butter two tablespoonfuls of flour. Add gradually to the boiling milk. Season highly with salt and pepper. Boil fifteen or twenty minutes. Dry the coral and sift it into the soup. Add enough of the water in which the bones were boiled to make it the proper thickness. Put the fat of the lobster into the tureen and pour the soup over it. Add one cup of lobster meat cut in small pieces.—[Miss H. L. Day.

Sali's Polish Soup.—Go into the garden and gather all kinds of young vegetables, carrots, string and shell beans, small peas, pod and all, young onions, a bit of celery and a sprig of parsley. This makes a good combination. Cut a few potatoes into inch cubes, add to the other vegetables cut up, and boil till they are tender. Add a tablespoonful of butter rubbed smooth with a tablespoonful of flour, salt and pepper to taste. Serve with croutons made by buttering stale bread and cutting it in inch squares and browning in a slow oven.—[Amy L. Handy.

Fish

KEDGEREE.—Put one cupful of boiled rice and one-half pound shredded codfish in a baking dish. Make a sauce by melting one tablespoonful of butter and one of flour in a saucepan, add one cup of milk, stir till thick, add the yolks of two hard boiled eggs rubbed through a sieve and a little salt and pepper. Pour this over the fish and rice; stand in the oven till hot.—[* * * * * *

FISH SOUFFLE.—Cook one cup of bread crumbs in one-half cup of milk. Take from the fire and add the yolks of two eggs, a little salt and pepper and one cup of shredded codfish. When well mixed stir in carefully the whites of two eggs beaten to a dry froth. Put quickly into a baking dish and bake five minutes in a quick oven. Serve at once.—[* * * * *

SCALLOPED FISH.—One and one-half cups cold flaked fish, three-quarters cup milk and a large piece of butter. Thicken with two tablespoonfuls of flour, add a pinch of salt and a little pepper, a little Worcestershire sauce, juice of one-half a lemon and the yolk of one egg. Cover the fish with cracker crumbs and bits of butter and bake in ramkins. Serve very hot.—[Grace B. Holway.

ON CAPE COD

GREAT-GRANDMOTHER'S RED FISH.—Equal parts of cold potatoes, cold boiled beets and salt codfish that has been freshened. Chop altogether like fine hash. Heat in a spider with a generous lump of butter, a little pepper and a little milk, not enough to make it liquid.—[Miss Lucia Howard.

A SALT CODFISH DINNER.—Two pounds "Not a Bone" codfish, one dozen large potatoes, six onions, six beets, half a pound of salt pork. Soak the fish in cold water two hours then boil it half an hour. Boil the beets separately, boil the onions in a bag with the potatoes. Cut the pork in small squares and fry to extract the fat. Serve all hot. What is left can be minced and fried next day.—[Mrs. Job C. Cobb.

BAKED FILLET OF SOLE.—One dozen "Slivers." Dip each in corn meal and roll up and fasten with a small skewer or wooden toothpick, stand them in a baking pan and lay a small piece of salt pork on each one. Bake in a quick oven till done. Make a brown gravy in the pan to serve with them.—[Mrs. E. A. Handy.

TURBOT A LA CREME.—Use either haddock or halibut. Boil about three pounds of fish until done. Remove the bones and skin and flake. Make the following sauce: Put one pint of milk in double boiler, half an onion, chopped, parsley, salt and pepper. When the milk boils add two tablespoonfuls of flour that has been stirred smooth with a little cold milk, butter the size of a large egg and the juice of a lemon. Cook until it thickens and strain through a gravy strainer over the fish. Put in buttered baking dish. Cover with crumbs and butter and bake.—[Mrs. S. L. Bartlett.

Codfish Balls.—Two cups of codfish picked in small pieces, one quart of potatoes cut small. Boil together till the potatoes are just done; drain well and mash. Add half a tablespoonful of butter, one well beaten egg and a little pepper. Beat all together till light and creamy; if it seems dry add a little cream. Form into balls and roll in flour. Fry in smoking hot deep fat. These can be made into cakes and fried in pork fat.—[Mrs. E. A. Handy.

Sauce Hollandaise.—Cream half a cup of butter, the yolks of two raw eggs beaten into the butter one at a time, a dash of cayenne pepper, a little salt, juice of one-half lemon and three-fourths cup of boiling water, added gradually stirring all the time. Cook in a double boiler till of the right consistency. Be careful it does not curdle.—[* * * *

Codfish Chops.—Cook two tablespoonfuls of chopped onion in two tablespoonfuls of butter three minutes; add two tablespoonfuls of flour and stir till smooth, add two cups of boiling water and cook till thick. Add one cup of shredded codfish, half a teaspoonful of made mustard, and a little white pepper, one egg, and cook for a minute stirring all the time. When cold form into the shape of cutlets or croquettes; roll in sifted bread crumbs, then in slightly beaten egg to which has been added a little salt and one tablespoonful of water, then again in crumbs. Fry and serve hot.—[* * * *

Shellfish

VIRGINIA BROILED LOBSTER.—Split live lobsters with a sharp knife. Remove the poison vein from the tail and crack the claws. Bake in a baking pan in a hot oven one-half hour. Serve with melted butter.—[Mrs. Peterson.

OYSTER PIE.—Line a deep dish with pie crust. Have one quart of oysters drained. Put a layer of oysters in the dish, a thin layer of cracker crumbs with some small pieces of butter dotted over. Then another layer of oysters, crackers, butter; continue until the dish is nearly full. Mix the liquor from the oysters with a little salt and pepper and cream; pour this over the pie and put on the top crust and bake in a moderate oven till brown.—[* * * *

MACARONI AND CLAMS.—One-half pound macaroni boiled tender; one pint of clams, one slice of onion, one tablespoonful of butter, one tablespoonful of flour, one cup rich milk. Drain the clams and chop them. Scald the clam liquor and onion and skim it. Melt the butter and stir in the flour till smooth, then add milk and cook till it thickens, add clam liquor and cook a minute. Put layers of macaroni and chopped clams in a baking dish, pour over the sauce and bake about twenty minutes. This is extremely good made with oysters instead of clams.—[Mrs. E. A. Handy.

PICKLED OYSTERS.—Put a cup of cold water into a sauce pan with a cup of vinegar, let it boil up and skim. Cook oysters in it till plump, then take them out and add a little sugar and whole spices, cloves and alspice. Boil a few minutes and pour it over the oysters. Serve cold for tea. Use three pints of oysters for this quantity.—[Mrs. Ruth E. Chipman.

SCALLOPED SCALLOPS.—Melt butter the size of half an egg in the bottom of baking dish. Next put a layer of crumbs, a layer of scallops, pepper, salt and butter. Repeat this until the dish is full. Make a hole in the middle with spoon and pour milk in gradually until it covers the scallops. Have the top layer crumbs and dot with butter. Don't be afraid of the milk if you want them good. I never use cream.—[F. G. Phinney.

DANIEL WEBSTER'S CLAM CHOWDER.—Two quarts of clams. Separate the bags from the shoulders. Strain off the liquor to settle. Chop the heads and shoulders quite fine. Pare and slice eight potatoes. Cut up a good-sized slice of pork and fry out. Eight hard crackers soaked. Throw into the kettle chopped clams, a little salt and pepper, then a layer of potatoes. Pour over the strained liquor, then add sufficient cold water to quite cover the whole. Cook until the potatoes are done, then add the soft part of the clams, crackers, one pint of milk. Boil eight minutes and serve hot. Onions if you like.—[Mrs. Barney Davis.

CLAM FRITTERS.—One quart of clams drained and chopped fine, half a cup of clam water, half a cup of cream, two well beaten eggs (three are better), two cups of flour and a little pepper. Fry like pan cakes in half an inch of pork fat.—[Mrs. E. A. Handy.

ON CAPE COD

Oyster Chowder.—Two slices of fat salt pork, cut in dice, one onion sliced thin, one pint oysters, one pint potatoes cut as for French fried, one quart very rich milk, one-half cup fine cracker crumbs, salt and pepper. Fry the pork and onions together but do not let them brown. Cook the oysters in their own liquor until just plump and add the pork, onion and potatoes that have been boiled till tender. Mix in the cracker crumbs and hot milk. Let the chowder stand where it will not cook for half an hour. This "ripens" it and brings out the flavor.—[Mrs. E. A. Handy.

Yacht Oyster Soup.—Two quarts of milk, one head of celery, one-half pound of butter, one cup of rolled crackers, salt, a pinch of red pepper. Boil the milk with the celery, strain off the celery, set the milk back on the stove, add the butter and the seasoning, one hundred small oysters. Let it simmer a little till the edges of the oysters curl. Thicken with the cracker and serve at once. Old-fashioned receipt.—[Grace B. Holway.

Broiled Oysters.—One egg, cracker crumbs, and one pint of oysters. Dip the oysters in the egg and then in the cracker crumbs and broil over a clear fire. Make a dressing of one pint of milk and one teaspoonful of flour, salt and pepper and butter the size of an egg. Boil up once and pour over the oysters.—[Grace B. Holway.

Stuffed Oysters, a Southern Dish.—Fry one small onion chopped fine and a little parsley in one tablespoonful of butter. Wash and drain one quart of oysters and chop with two slices of toast, season with salt and red pepper, mix with the onion and cook until it does not taste raw. Fill shells with a mixture, cover with cracker crumbs and butter. Bake till brown.

Oyster Shortcake.—Make a good biscuit crust, roll out in two rounds. Put one in the pan and spread with soft butter, put the other one on top and bake. Cook one quart of oysters in their own liquor, drain and keep the oysters hot. Make a sauce of one tablespoonful of butter and two of flour melted together, add the oyster liquor and one cup of cream, cook till thick, stirring all the time. Add the oysters. Split the shortcake and put the creamed oysters between the layers and on top.—[Mrs. E. A. Handy.

Cape Cod Clam Chowder.—One quart of clams thoroughly cleaned, one quart of milk, one good sized onion, six potatoes, four slices of pork, one tablespoonful of butter, three crackers broken, pepper. Fry out the pork and then put in the sliced onion and cook a few minutes; put them into a large kettle and add the sliced potatoes; boil them till soft in water to cover them; add the clam water (after straining), then the clams. Cook five minutes, then add the quart of milk, and when it comes to a boil add butter, cracker and pepper. Enough for six or eight persons.—[Mrs. E. D. Crocker.

Meats

Planked Steak.—Rub a two-inch plank with olive oil to prevent its burning and heat it in the oven for half an hour. Put the steak on the plank and put in a hot oven for ten minutes, turn steak, butter well and cook ten minutes more, add more butter and a little salt and serve on the plank. This is for steak one inch thick. —[Mrs. E. A. Handy.

Chicken Terrapin.—Chop a cold roast chicken and one parboiled sweetbread moderately fine. Make a rich cream sauce with one cup hot cream and one-quarter cup of butter and two tablespoonfuls of flour. Add the chicken and sweetbread, pepper and salt to taste. Heat it over hot water fifteen minutes and just before serving add the yolks of two well beaten eggs and one wine glass of sherry. Serve at once.—[Grace B. Holway.

Begorra.—One pint of cold lamb, minced; six or seven sticks of macaroni cooked tender. Put in a buttered baking dish with one cup of stewed tomato, a little pepper and salt and three tablespoonfuls of gravy. Cover with crumbs and bits of butter and bake.—[Mrs. S. L. Bartlett.

Mrs. Trowbridge's Breakfast Bacon.—Slice fat bacon and lay it in milk for ten minutes; dip it in flour and fry it in its own fat. Take out when crisp and fry cold potatoes in the fat. Serve on platter with potatoes in the middle and bacon on outer circle.—[Mrs. L. Mortimer.

Roast Ham.—Wash and trim a small ham, soak over night. In the morning cover the entire ham thickly with a flour and water paste, put it in a dripping pan and bake four hours. Do not baste it and do not be frightened if it looks as if it were burning to a cinder. This will cut in thin slices and be perfectly tender and much more digestible than boiled ham.—[Mrs. E. A. Handy.

Sausage Crisps.—Make a batter of three well beaten eggs, level teaspoonful of salt, two cups of milk and two-thirds of a cup of flour. Mix the flour with a little of the milk before stirring into the batter to prevent its lumping. Spread a thin layer of sausage meat on the bottom of a baking pan and pour the well beaten batter over it. Bake in a hot oven till brown. Serve hot. This is very rich and very good on a cold day.—[Mrs. E. A. Handy.

*Frizzled Beef.—Half a pound of smoked beef cut in thin shavings. Pour boiling water over it and let it stand ten minutes. Drain, and heat it in one tablespoonful of hot butter, to curl or frizzle it. Add one cup of hot cream; or make a sauce with one cup of milk, one tablespoonful of butter and one tablespoonful of flour; pour it over one well beaten egg, add the beef and a little pepper, and serve at once. Or, frizzle it and mix with two or three poached eggs.—[Mrs. E. S. Phinney.

*From Midsummer Cook Book.

LAMB SOUFFLE.—Melt half a tablespoonful of butter and add one-half tablespoonful of flour, one-half teaspoonful of salt, one-half teaspoonful of celery salt, a few drops of onion juice and a few grains of pepper. Then add gradually one cup of scalded milk and one-quarter cup of stale bread crumbs. Remove from the fire and add one cup of finely chopped cold lamb. Add the well beaten yolks of two eggs and last fold in the whites of two eggs beaten stiffly. Bake in a moderate oven and serve with tomato sauce.—[Mrs. Tripp.

*VEAL BIRDS.—Take slices of veal from the loin cut very thin. Wipe them, remove the bone, skin and fat, and pound until they are one-quarter of an inch thick. Trim into pieces two and one-half inches by four. Chop the trimmings fine with one square inch of fat salt pork for each bird. Add one-half as much fine cracker crumbs as there is meat; season highly with salt, pepper, thyme, lemon, cayenne and onion to taste. Moisten with a raw egg and a little hot water. Spread the mixture on each slice and roll tightly, tie or fasten with a skewer. Dredge with salt, pepper and flour. Fry slowly in hot butter until the birds are a golden brown; then half cover with cream and simmer till they are tender. Remove the strings or skewers and serve on toast. Garnish with parsley and lemon. If the veal used seems tough dip the slices in olive oil before spreading with the stuffing.—[Miss E. Munroe.

*BEEF LOAF.—Chop one and one-half pounds beefsteak very fine; add two cups rolled crackers, one cup cold water, one-half cup butter, with salt and pepper. Shape into a loaf, place in pan, and bake slowly two hours. To be sliced when cold.—[Miss D. E. Hinckley.

*From Midsummer Cook Book.

*A LA MODE MUTTON.—Make a dressing as for turkey. Fill two large or four small onions with whole cloves. Take a leg of mutton; take out the bone; put in the stuffing; place it in pot on a grate; put in the onions; dredge with flour; add two tablespoonfuls allspice, two cloves, two peppers and quite a lot of salt. Add enough water to allow the meat to rest on it, keeping the same quantity through the cooking. Steam, for a large leg, seven hours. Keep the pot covered tight all the time. Gravy: take some of the liquor from the pot; add currant jelly and a little wine and serve.—[Miss Julia G. Davis.

*DELICIOUS STUFFING FOR FOWL.—Two dozen oysters chopped very fine, mixed with two cups of fine bread or cracker crumbs, a full ounce of butter, a tablespoonful of chopped parsley, a little grated lemon peel, plenty of salt and black pepper, a little red pepper, and one tablespoonful of chopped celery. Moisten with a little oyster liquor, a little cream and the well beaten yolk of an egg.—[Miss M. L. Bacon.

*QUEEN'S MOUTHFULS.—Mince very fine one pound veal, poultry or game, cooked or raw, with a little fat salt pork. Add salt, pepper, nutmeg, parsley, a little onion, a few bread crumbs and two eggs. Put all in a saucepan with two tablespoonfuls of cream and two ounces butter. Stir over the fire for five minutes. Let the mixture get cold. Roll out some light paste the thickness of a dollar. Cut out some rounds three inches in diameter. Lay in a little of the meat, cover with another round and press the edges together. Bake in a rather hot oven.—[E. J. H.

*From Midsummer Cook Book.

ON CAPE COD

*Chicken Pilaf.—Boil a fowl until tender; when cold cut in not too small pieces. Pilaf: One cup of rice, one can of tomatoes, a large piece of butter; cook in a farina kettle for an hour and a half. Ten minutes before serving add the chicken. —[Mrs. Ellen Davis.

Baked Sausages. — Prick sausages and cover with boiling water for ten minutes; remove and put into cold water for two minutes. Roll in beaten egg and then in bread crumbs; put in a pan in a hot oven ten minutes. This rule is for sausages in cases.—[* * * *

*Veal Loaf.—Three pounds of raw veal and one-half pound of salt pork chopped together very fine, six or eight crackers rolled fine, three well beaten eggs, one-half cup of thick cream, one-quarter of a pound of butter, one glass of sherry and one of brandy or port wine, one onion chopped fine and the juice and grated rind of one lemon, one teaspoonful each of pepper, cloves, sweet marjoram, sage and salt. Mix these all together with the meat and mould into a loaf; place in a dripping pan, cover the top with more cracker crumbs and bits of butter; add a little water to the pan. While baking baste often with melted butter.—[Miss M. L. Bacon.

Sauce for Game.—Six tablespoonfuls of currant jelly, two tablespoonfuls of butter melted together, add two tablespoonfuls of lemon juice; just before taking from the fire add one tablespoonful of grated orange peel and one glass of port wine. Cool a little and serve with venison or any kind of game.—[Mrs. E. A. Handy.

*From Midsummer Cook Book.

Smothered Fowl and Oysters.—Dress a good plump fowl as for roasting. Drain one pint of oysters and fill the fowl; sew up and set in a kettle to steam, put a rack under it to keep it out of the water. Put salt, pepper and some pieces of celery in the water. Boil hard until the fowl is tender but not broken. Serve with a sauce made from the water in the kettle and one cup of cream thickened with flour. Add one pint of oysters and cook till they curl. Pour this over the fowl. An Old-fashioned Rule.

*Chicken Terrapin.—Boil a fowl with the giblets until tender. When cold, cut fowl and giblets into small pieces. Put in a saucepan piece of butter, not quite quarter of a pound, with a tablespoonful of flour; thoroughly mix. Add three hard boiled eggs chopped very fine, a cup of broth, a cup of cream, salt and pepper. Simmer for ten minutes, add chicken, thoroughly heat, when ready to serve, a cup of wine. Truffles improve the terrapin.—[Mrs. Ellen Davis.

Savory Beef.—Four or five pounds of round of beef or any inexpensive cut. Fry till very brown all over; this will take about half an hour. Put the beef in a covered dish not much larger than the beef. Mix two tablespoons of flour with the fat in the pan the meat was fried in. If there is not fat enough add a little butter. When the flour browns pour in a quart of water and boil till thick. Add salt and one teaspoon of kitchen bouquet. Have an onion and carrot sliced over the meat. Add some parsley and celery salt; pour the gravy over it and bake in the oven four hours, adding water if it cooks away. This is easily adapted to the fireless cooker.—[Mrs. E. A. Handy.

*From Midsummer Cook Book.

ON CAPE COD

*Pressed Chicken.—Boil two chickens tender, take out the bones and chop the meat fine. Add a small cup of bread crumbs; season to taste with butter, pepper, salt, and a little sage; pour in enough of the liquor to make it moist; mould in any shape you choose, and when cold cut in slices.—[Mrs. Danforth Parker.

Home-made Corned Beef.—Put five or six pounds of fresh beef into a kettle, the brisket is the best piece to use. Add one cup of salt, one tablespoon sugar and a few whole spices, about half a teaspoonful. Pour over this two quarts or more of boiling water and boil slowly until very tender. If the water boils away add more to keep two quarts in the kettle. This is especially good done in the fireless cooker.—[Mrs. E. A. Handy.

Plain Southern Okra.—Take a chicken and cut in pieces to fry. Have your spider hot with lard in it to cook the chicken. Flour each piece and cook to a good brown. Put your chicken in a soup pot. Cut up one large onion in slices and one pint of okra; fry brown in the fat in which the chicken was cooked. When done pour all the contents of the spider into the soup pot with the chicken and add five tomatoes cut up, three ears of corn cut from the cob, one cup of lima beans and two quarts of water. Boil all together for three or four hours. Season with salt and pepper. Serve without straining.—[Miss Mary K. Cobb.

Veal Fricassee.—Cut the veal in pieces and roll in cracker crumbs. Melt a small piece of butter or lard in a frying pan and cook veal in it. When the veal is done make a gravy in the pan with a little flour and milk to pour over it.—[Mrs. Ruth E. Chipman.

Baked Liver.—Take a whole calf's liver, make stuffing as for turkey, tie in the liver, bake an hour and a half, cook strips of bacon on the liver. Serve with broiled tomatoes.—[Mrs. Ellen M. Davis.

*From Midsummer Cook Book.

Vegetables

*Corn Pudding.—Eight good-sized ears of corn, scored and scraped, two eggs well beaten with a bowl of milk, a little salt and a good-sized piece of butter. Bake an hour in a good oven. —[Mrs. Ruth E. Chipman.

*Carrots.—Scrape young carrots and boil half an hour; slice and stew in one cup of hot water and one tablespoonful of butter, a little pepper and salt. When soft add four tablespoonfuls of cream, one tablespoonful of butter cut in bits and rolled in flour. —Miss M. L. Bacon.

Hominy Puff.—Two cups hot boiled hominy, one-quarter cup of butter, one-half cup of milk, four eggs. Stir the butter, milk and the yolks of the eggs into the hot hominy, last of all add the whites of the eggs beaten stiff. Bake half an hour.—[Mrs. E. A. Handy.

*Baked Sweet Potatoes.—Twelve sweet potatoes boiled soft, one-half cup of butter, one-half cup of sugar. Slice the potatoes and arrange in layers in bread pan. Have the top layer sugar. Add a little water to keep moist. Bake till done.—[J. B. G.

*From Midsummer Cook Book.

ON CAPE COD

Corn Fritters.—One well beaten egg, three ears of corn grated from the cob, two tablespoonfuls of flour, one tablespoonful of milk, more or less according to the juiciness of the corn, a pinch of salt. Drop mixture by teaspoonfuls into boiling fat about an inch deep.

Italian Macaroni.—Cook one-half pound of macaroni in one quart of soup stock or beef extract and water until tender. Put two tablespoonfuls of butter and one chopped onion in a frying pan and fry till a golden brown. Add one cup of chopped ham and the same of chicken, some mushrooms if you have them; when hot season with salt, pepper, one tablespoonful of Worcestershire sauce and two of tomato sauce. Pour it into a shallow dish and sprinkle grated cheese over the top. Set into the oven till it begins to brown. This is a good luncheon dish and no other meat is needed.—[* * * *

Sauce for Spaghetti.—Cook one medium sized onion, minced, in two tablespoonfuls of butter till soft, then rub in two tablespoonfuls of flour gradually. Add two cups of tomatoes slowly, stirring constantly. When smooth and thick remove from the fire and strain. Reheat and add one-half a teaspoonful each of allspice, clove and cinnamon; pour over cooked spaghetti. Serve with grated cheese.—[Mrs. Vaughan Bacon.

German Puffers.—Peel and grate several raw potatoes and drain. To each cupful of potato add one well beaten egg, and salt and pepper and one tablespoonful of cream. Fry like pancakes in plenty of fat.—[Mrs. E. A. Handy.

Escalloped Potatoes.—Put in a deep pudding dish a layer of raw potatoes peeled and sliced very thin, season with salt and pepper and bits of butter; continue these layers till the dish is full. Cover with milk and bake until done. If cheese is liked, sprinkle over the top before baking.—[* * * *

Candied Sweet Potatoes.—Peel and slice raw sweet potatoes. Melt two tablespoonfuls of butter and two of sugar in a frying pan and add the potatoes with a little water; cover and cook till they begin to be tender, then put them in the oven uncovered to brown. —[Mrs. E. A. Handy.

Stuffed Potatoes.—Bake good-sized potatoes until just done. Cut off one end and scoop out the potato; do not break the skins. Mash well and season with salt and pepper, add a little cream and whip light; put back into the shells and brown in the oven. —[* * * *

*Spaghetti. An Italian receipt brought from Palermo.—Take a quart of rich beef soup; mix it with half a can of tomato or an equal amount of fresh tomatoes. Boil them together and then strain so as to rid the soup of pulp and seed; season with pepper and salt. Put a roll of spaghetti into the soup. Do not break the sticks; by putting in one end of the sticks to the boiling soup, it will gradually all bend in. Boil until all of the soup is absorbed by the spaghetti. Just before serving it, sprinkle thoroughly with grated Parmesan cheese. To have a perfect dish, buy your spaghetti from the Italian dealers. Also do not use the bottled cheese. It can be obtained from the Italian dealers; grate it as it is needed. It keeps a long time.—[Mrs. W. R. Ellis.

*From Midsummer Cook Book.

ON CAPE COD

German Noodles.—One egg, as much water as the egg shell will hold. Mix the egg and water, add a little salt. Stir in as much flour as possible and work smooth on the bread board; break off small pieces and roll as thin as paper. Lay them on cloths to dry for an hour, roll up and cut in quarter inch ribbons. Dry and use like maccaroni. It is much better.—[Mrs. E. A. Handy.

Spaghetti, Italian Style.—Boil one-half of a package of spaghetti till tender; put in a buttered dish and pour over the following sauce: Fry one tablespoonful of onion in one tablespoonful of butter; when well browned add one large tablespoonful of flour. Add gradually one and a half cups of tomato, salt. Grate cheese over the top and cover with crumbs and bake.—[Mrs. S. L. Bartlett.

Potato Turnovers.—One pint of freshly mashed potato; add one well beaten egg, one tablespoonful of flour, and salt and pepper to taste. Roll out on a well floured board and cut in squares. Put a spoonful of chopped meat on each square and fold over like a turnover. Bake long enough to heat the meat and brown the potato. Serve with tomato sauce or brown gravy.—[Mrs. E. A. Handy.

Smothered Potatoes.—Six potatoes and one onion peeled and sliced thin. Put two slices of fat salt pork cut in dice in a frying pan, when it begins to fry add the potatoes and onion with a very little water. Cover tight and cook, turning gently once in a while. When the potatoes are soft take off the cover and cook away the water and brown. Turn out on a platter and serve. It will take about one hour to cook and brown.—[Mrs. E. A. Handy.

Salads and Salad Dressings

Cream Salad Dressing, German.—Whip one-half cup of cream, either sweet or sour, add one-half teaspoonful of salt, a little black pepper. Mix two teaspoonfuls of grated onion to two tablespoonfuls of vinegar and beat into the cream. This is good with all kinds of vegetable salad.—[Mrs. E. A. Handy.

Quick Tomato Jelly.—Heat two cups of any good chili sauce with half a cup of water and strain over one tablespoonful of gelatine softened in one-quarter of a cup of cold water. Stir till dissolved and pour into moulds. When hard serve with mayonnaise on lettuce.—[Mrs. B. D. Peterson, Jr.

Boiled Salad Dressing.—Mix the yolks of three eggs, three tablespoonfuls of vinegar, half a teaspoonful of salt and the same of mustard and a little red pepper; cook in double boiler till thick and creamy, stir all the time to prevent curdling. Add one tablespoonful of butter as soon as it is thick and while it is hot. When ready to serve add the whites of the eggs beaten to a dry froth.

Potato Salad.—Cut cold boiled potatoes in small pieces, add celery cut small. Put a layer of potatoes and one of celery in the salad bowl in a little chopped onion and parsley. Pour over a boiled dressing.—[* * * *

Quick Mayonnaise.—One teaspoonful of dry mustard, one-half teaspoonful of salt, one cup of olive oil, juice of half a lemon, one egg. Mix the mustard, salt and lemon juice, add the slightly beaten yolk of egg and stir well. Add the oil drop by drop until you have used one teaspoonful, then beat with an egg-beater adding the oil a teaspoonful at a time and as it mixes add the oil by tablespoonfuls. When all the oil is used add the white of the egg beaten stiff. The ingredients should be cold.—[Mrs. E. A. Handy.

Russian Salad.—One can of French peas, twice as much celery, cut in dice; same quantity of carrot; one tablespoonful of chopped parsley. Serve with mayonnaise dressing.—[Mrs. Charles Knowles.

Crackers to Serve with Salad.—Split Boston crackers and soak in cold water for ten minutes, remove carefully into a tin plate, put a lump of butter on each one. Place in a hot oven for twenty minutes. Add a little cheese if liked.—[Mrs. B. Davis.

German Potato Salad, Hot. —Cut potatoes in inch cubes and boil till tender, drain and add one thinly sliced onion, salt and pepper. Make the dressing while the potatoes are cooking. Fry four thick slices of bacon cut in dice till crisp, add one-quarter cup of vinegar and let it get hot, pour over the potatoes and onions and serve at once.—[Mrs. E. A. Handy.

Sweet Potato Salad.—Cut boiled sweet potatoes in cubes, one-third as much raw apple cut fine and a little celery, nuts if liked. Serve with mayonnaise dressing.—[Mrs. F. H. Thayer.

Halibut Salad.—Equal parts of cold boiled halibut and cold hard boiled eggs or potatoes diced. Arrange on lettuce leaves and cover with a good salad dressing. Chopped olives can be added.—[Mrs. Leslie Jones.

Salad Dressing.—Put two-thirds of a cup of vinegar, a piece of butter the size of an egg, a saltspoonful of salt and a speck of pepper into a saucepan and set on the stove to boil. Mix two tablespoonfuls of sugar, a quarter of a teaspoonful of mustard and a heaping teaspoonful of cornstarch together thoroughly, add a half cup of cream, and when free from lumps pour slowly into the boiling vinegar. Stir till smooth and thick, remove from the fire and pour the mixture over the well beaten yolks of three eggs and beat for five minutes. Strain the juice of a large lemon, add it to the dressing and beat well again.—[Mrs. Lottie C. Holmes.

"To be a good cook means the knowledge of all herbs, balms and spices; and of all that is healing and sweet in fields and groves, savory in meats. It means carefulness, inventiveness, watchfulness, intelligence and readiness of appliances. It means the economy of your great-grand-mothers and the science of modern chemists; it means English thoroughness, French art and Arabian hospitality; it means, in fine, that you are to be perfectly and always ladies (loaf givers), and you are to see that everybody has something nice to eat."—[Ruskin.

Eggs, Cheese and Sandwiches

Egg Timbale.—Break six eggs into a bowl, add one cup of milk and a little salt and pepper, beat until creamy, and pour into buttered cups. Stand the cups in a pan of hot water and bake till set. Turn out on a platter and serve with a cream sauce poured round them.—[* * * *

Good Omelet.—Six eggs beaten separately, one-half cup of milk, a pinch of salt added to the yolks. Stir the whites in lightly and bake in a moderate oven.—[Mrs. F. H. Thayer.

Cheese Souffle.—Make a cream sauce of two tablespoonfuls of butter, one of flour and one-half cup of milk, season with salt and cayenne, add the beaten yolks of three eggs and one cupful of grated cheese. When cool add the whites of four eggs beaten very light. Bake in a buttered dish one-half hour; do not have the oven too hot.—[* * * *

Breakfast Eggs.—Break two eggs in an egg cup for each person. Add a teaspoonful of cream, a little salt and pepper. Set cups in a saucepan of hot water, cover and cook till the whites are set. Serve in the cups at once.—[Mrs. E. A. Handy.

Omelet.—Melt one tablespoonful of butter, stir in one tablespoonful of flour, add one cup of milk, stir and cook until thick, cool for a few minutes and add to the beaten yolks of five eggs. Beat the whites until so dry that you can turn the bowl over without spilling; mix lightly with the yolks and cream sauce. Melt one tablespoonful of butter in a frying pan and when hot turn in the omelet. Cook a few minutes and then set the pan in the oven to finish. Be careful not to cook too long. This will serve five people.—[Mrs. E. A. Handy.

Oyster Sandwiches.—One quart of oysters, chopped fine, add one-half cup of butter, one beaten egg, one-half cup of cracker crumbs, salt, pepper and a dash of cayenne. Cook very lightly, stirring with a fork. Use to fill sandwiches when cold.—[* * *

Cheese Fondue.—Mix one cup of scalded milk, one cup of soft bread crumbs, one-quarter of a pound of mild cheese cut in small pieces, one tablespoonful of butter and a half teaspoonful of salt. Add the well beaten yolks of three eggs, and last the whites of the eggs beaten stiff. Bake in buttered dish twenty or thirty minutes in a moderate oven.—[Miss Mary Cobb.

Cheese Filling for Timbals.—Melt half a pound of American cheese with one tablespoon butter. When smooth add two well-beaten eggs and half a cup of thin cream, salt and pepper. Cook until smooth and thick. Fill timbal cases or serve on crackers. This is very good made in the chafing dish and served on toast. It will not get stringy and tough. If some is left over it makes a good cold cheese filling for sandwiches.—[Mrs. E. A. Handy.

Fried Cheese Sandwiches.—Put a slice of cheese between two slices of bread and soak in a batter made of one slightly beaten egg and one-half cup of milk and a little salt. Fry in butter.—[Mrs. E. A. Handy.

Mock Cheese Souffle.—Butter slices of stale bread and put a layer in a baking dish. Cover with thin slices of cheese or grated cheese, repeat the bread and butter and cheese until the dish is full. Beat two eggs light and add two cups of milk, a level teaspoon salt and a dash of red pepper. Pour this over the bread and cheese; let it stand half an hour. Bake half an hour and serve at once.—[Mrs. E. A. Handy.

For the Chafing Dish

Al Crocker's Welsh Rarebit.—Put a piece of butter the size of an egg in the chafing dish. Cut one pound of soft cheese in small pieces and add to the butter; when all begins to melt pour in mixture containing two well beaten eggs, half a teaspoonful of mustard, dry, saltspoonful of salt, half a saltspoonful of cayenne. When thoroughly melted and mixed add one-third of a bottle of beer. This must be stirred constantly till done, when it will be smooth and creamy. Serve on crackers.

Lobster Newburg.—One and a half cups of lobster meat, one-quarter of a cup of sherry, one-quarter of a cup of butter, three tablespoonfuls of flour, one and three-quarters cups of cream, one-half tablespoonful of brandy, pinch of salt. Let lobster stand in sherry fifteen minutes, add the butter and cook five minutes, add the other ingredients, cook and serve hot.—[Mrs. B. Davis.

Pigs in Blankets.—Season large oysters with salt and pepper, roll in very thin slices of fat bacon and fasten with a toothpick. Fry in a hot pan until the bacon is done, or run six on a silver skewer and broil till the bacon is crisp.—[Mrs. E. A. Handy.

ON CAPE COD

TOMATO RAREBIT.—One cup of stewed and strained tomato, two well beaten eggs, one tablespoonful of butter, one cup of cheese cut in small pieces, salt and a dash of cayenne. Melt butter and cheese together, add tomato and seasoning, cook till it is smooth, add the eggs and cook until like thick custard. Serve at once on hot buttered toast.—[Mrs. E. A. Handy.

SHERRY ROAST.—Melt one tablespoonful of butter in the chafing dish, add one saltspoonful of salt and a dash of paprika, half a cup of finely cut celery and twenty-five oysters. Cook until the oysters curl, then add a wine glass of sherry, heat and serve on toast.—[Mrs. E. A. Handy.

CURRIED OYSTERS.—Put one tablespoonful of butter, one teaspoonful of grated onion, one-half teaspoonful of curry powder and one tablespoonful of flour in a hot chafing dish. When blended add the oyster liquor and cook a minute, stirring. Add the oysters and when they curl serve on toast.—[Mrs. E. A. Handy.

OYSTERS AND TOMATOES.—Two tablespoonfuls of butter, one tablespoonful of flour, one slice of onion, one cup of stewed and strained tomatoes, one pint of oysters, salt and pepper. Cook the onion in the butter till light brown, add the flour and brown again. Add the tomatoes and cook and stir until thick. Add the oysters, drained, and cook until they plump up. Serve on toast.—[Mrs. E. A. Handy.

BEEF STEAK WITH OYSTERS.—Broil the steak, cover the top with raw oysters and set it on the grate of the oven till the oysters curl. Serve at once.—[Mrs. E. A. Handy.

Meat Warmed in Gravy.—Cut any cold meat in small pieces; for three cups of meat take one cup of gravy or stock; failing that, one teaspoonful of beef extract and one cup of hot water. Season highly with salt, pepper and a little onion juice if liked. When this gravy is hot stir in one teaspoonful of cornstarch, wet with a little cold water; when it boils add the meat and heat thoroughly but do not let it boil as that will toughen the meat.—[Mrs. E. A. Handy.

Chicken and Oysters.—Melt two tablespoonfuls of butter, add two tablespoonfuls of flour; cook and stir till smooth, add two cups of cream and cook till thick and smooth. Add one pint of oysters that have been cooked in their own liquor and drained; one pint of cold chicken cut in small pieces, salt and pepper, and a wine glass of sherry. Heat and serve on hot buttered toast.—[Mrs. E. A. Handy.

Lobster a la Newburg.—For six or eight persons use the meat of a lobster weighing four pounds. One-half pint of cream, four tablespoonfuls of butter, two tablespoonfuls of brandy, two of sherry, half teaspoonful of salt, a little cayenne, a little nutmeg, yolks of two eggs. Cut lobster into small pieces, put butter in pan; when hot put in lobster, cook slowly five minutes. Then add brandy, sherry, salt and pepper and simmer three minutes. Beat yolks well, add the cream, pour over and stir constantly a minute and a half or until the cream thickens. Serve at once.—[Mrs. T. C. Day.

ON CAPE COD

Eggs Poached in Broth.—One pint of chicken or beef broth well seasoned. Bring to a boil, move the saucepan where it will be hot but not boil. Break in six eggs, be careful not to break the yolks. When the whites are set take them out of the broth and put them on hot buttered toast. Thicken the broth with two small teaspoonfuls of cornstarch wet with a little cold water. Boil up and pour over the eggs and toast.—[Mrs. E. A. Handy.

Poached Eggs in Milk.—Have plenty of milk scalding hot but not boiling, a little salt. Drop eggs in, being careful not to break the yolks. Keep the milk hot and as soon as the whites are set serve on toast. A good variation is to use thin cream and pour it over the toast carefully before taking out the eggs. The eggs should not be over twenty-four hours old.—[Mrs. E. A. Handy.

Tomato Eggs.—Cut three or four good-sized tomatoes into halves; take out a little of the inside, lay them in a pan containing two ounces of melted butter and fry them lightly. When nearly done, drop into each piece of tomato a raw egg. Watch carefully until egg has set, then remove from the pan and lay upon a slice of buttered toast. Cut the toast neatly around the tomatoes. Dust each with a little salt and pepper.—[Mrs. W. R. Ellis.

Puddings

INDIAN PUDDING.—One cup of corn meal, one-half cup of molasses, one quart of milk and a small piece of butter. Scald a little more than half the milk, stir in the meal, add the butter and the molasses and a little salt. Let it cool in a baking dish. Pour on the cold milk as you set it in the oven. Bake four hours.—[Mrs. Mary Freeman Hinckley.

SWEET POTATO PUDDING.—One cup of boiled and mashed sweet potato, two cups of hot milk, two well beaten eggs, three tablespoonfuls of sugar, one teaspoonful of cinnamon and nutmeg mixed, half a teaspoonful of salt. Bake in a buttered baking dish in a slow oven. Serve with cream.—[Mrs. E. A. Handy.

CRACKER PUDDING.—Add one well beaten egg to three tablespoonfuls of sugar. Two cups of milk, pinch of salt, three crackers rolled fine, nutmeg, and some seeded raisins. Bake about an hour and serve with butter and sugar.—[Mrs. F. H. Thayer.

CUSTARD BAKED PUDDING.—Three tablespoonfuls of flour, one pint of scalding milk, four eggs, yolks and whites beaten separately. Wet the flour in a little cold milk and add the hot milk, add the yolks and then the whites of the eggs. Bake twenty minutes and serve with sauce.

ON CAPE COD

PEACH COBBLER.—Butter the outside of a cup and insert it in the center of a buttered baking dish. Fill the dish with sliced peaches and one-half cup of sugar. Make a good biscuit crust, using two cups sifted flour, two teaspoonfuls of baking powder, a pinch of salt, four tablespoonfuls of butter rubbed into the flour, two eggs well beaten, add one and one-half cups of milk and stir all together. Roll out and cover the peaches. Bake one-half an hour in a moderate oven. Turn out the pudding on a deep platter and serve at once. The cup will be full of delicious syrup. Serve with whipped cream.—[Miss Grace B. Holway.

GRAHAM FRUIT PUDDING.—One and one-half cups sifted graham flour, one-half cup of molasses, one-quarter cup of melted butter, one-half cup of milk, one egg, one teaspoonful of soda, salt, a little spice, one-half cup of raisins and one-quarter citron. Steam in a buttered dish three hours.—[Mrs. F. H. Thayer.

PUDDING SAUCE.—Two cups of milk, one-half cup of sugar, two eggs and one teaspoonful of vanilla. Beat the eggs to a froth with the sugar, add slowly to the milk which should be boiling hot. Cook for a minute and serve.—[* * * *

BLUEBERRY DUMPLINGS.—Sift one quart of flour with four level teaspoonfuls of baking powder; mix with milk until it is as stiff as soft biscuit. Boil the berries first with a little water then add one-half cup each of sugar and molasses. Put the berries on to cook one hour before the dumplings are to be used. Cook forty minutes then drop in the dumplings, cook twenty minutes. Split and butter, pour the stewed berries over them.—[Mrs. Peterson.

Plum Pudding.—Half a pound of bread crumbs, one-quarter of a pound of beef suet or butter, one-half a pound of currants, one-half a pound of raisins, chopped, one-quarter of a pound of citron sliced thin, one-half teaspoonful of salt, four eggs, well beaten, one-half cup of milk, one-half cup of brandy or one cup of sherry, one-half cup of sugar. Cinnamon, mace and nutmeg. Boil four and a half hours. Serve with wine sauce.—[Miss Grace B. Holway.

Steamed Chocolate Pudding.—One-half cup of sugar, one teaspoonful of butter, one egg, one cup of flour sifted with one teaspoonful of baking powder, one square of chocolate, and half a cup of milk stirred in slowly. Steam one and one-quarter hours.—[Mrs. Leslie Jones.

Apple Pudding.—Six apples, two slices of bread, one cup of suet all chopped fine; juice of one lemon, a little salt, one teaspoonful of soda dissolved in a little water. Steam three hours. Serve with sauce.—[Mrs. Job C. Cobb.

Steamed Chocolate Pudding.—Cream three tablespoonfuls of butter, add three-quarters of a cup of sugar gradually and one well beaten egg. Mix and sift two and one-quarter cups of flour, four and one-half teaspoonfuls of baking powder and one-quarter teaspoonful of salt, add alternately with one cup of milk to first mixture, then add two and one-half squares of Baker's chocolate, melted. Turn into a buttered mould and steam two hours. Serve with cream sauce. Cream sauce: Cream one-quarter of a cup of butter, add one cup of powdered sugar gradually. Add drop by drop one-quarter cup of rich milk or cream, flavor with vanilla.—[Mrs. Maurice Hallett.

Black Pudding.—One cup of molasses, one-half cup of melted butter, one-half cup of sour milk, two cups of flour, one-half teaspoonful of soda, a little nutmeg and cinnamon. Steam one hour and serve with sauce. Sauce: One-half cup of butter creamed with one cup of sugar, one egg and one tablespoonful of vinegar. Steam over a teakettle.—[Mrs. F. H. Thayer.

Cold Sauce for Pudding.—One large tablespoonful of flour mixed with cold water till smooth, thicken with boiling water till the consistency of thick cream. When cold add half a cup of butter and one cup of sugar well creamed and a little vanilla. It should look curdled when served.—[Mrs. Leslie Jones.

Cold Desserts and Ices

Pineapple Sherbet.—One can of sliced pineapple, chopped fine, one pint of water, one pint of sugar, one tablespoonful of minute gelatine, juice of one lemon.—[Mrs. Thomas P. Lewis.

Lemon Cream.—Beat the yolks of four eggs with four tablespoonfuls of sugar, add the juice and grated rind of one large lemon and two tablespoonfuls of hot water. Simmer till it thickens then remove from the fire. Beat the whites of the eggs to a stiff froth with two tablespoonfuls of sugar and stir into the yolks previously cooked. To be eaten cold.—[Mrs. Job C. Cobb.

Raspberry or Strawberry Sherbet.—One pint of berry juice, one pint of sugar, one pint of water, one tablespoonful of gelatine, or one pint of preserved fruit, one cup of sugar, one quart of water, two lemons, one tablespoonful of gelatine. Soak the gelatine in a little of the water, cold, add the rest of the water hot to dissolve the gelatine. Add the other ingredients, cool and freeze.—[Mrs. F. H. Thayer.

Union Club Ice Cream.—One half a pound of sugar and three eggs beaten together to a cream. Boil a pint of cream and when cool add to the sugar and egg and cook in a double boiler till it is the consistency of thick custard.—[Miss Lucia Howard.

Mrs. M.'s Chocolate Ice Cream.—Four squares of chocolate put in a double boiler and entirely melted. Add one quart of milk, stir until dissolved. Beat three eggs, a pinch of salt and one and one-half cups of sugar together, cook with milk until it is thick. When cold add a pint of cream and one tablespoonful of vanilla. Freeze.—[Mrs. Lawrence Mortimer.

Lemon Cream.—Three lemons, four eggs, pint of boiling water, sugar to taste, about one cup full. Grate the lemons and pour the boiling water on the peel, let it stand a few minutes, add the sugar while hot and strain. Add the eggs well beaten. Stir well together and cook in a double boiler till it thickens.—[Miss H. L. Day.

Chocolate Sauce for Ice Cream.—Two tablespoonfuls of butter, one level tablespoonful of flour, four teaspoonfuls of cocoa, one cup of cold water, four tablespoonfuls of sugar, one teaspoonful of vanilla and a pinch of salt. Melt the butter, mix the flour and cocoa and stir into the butter, add the water gradually, stirring and beating all the time. Cook till it thickens and before serving add the sugar and vanilla.—[Mrs. Alfred Crocker, Jr.

Velvet Cream.—One-half box of gelatine, one and one-half cups of sherry, one lemon, grated rind and juice, one and one-half cups of sugar, one and one-half pints of cream. Soak the gelatine in the wine, add the lemon and sugar. Heat all together until dissolved. Strain and cool, when nearly cold enough to stiffen add the cream whipped. Pour into moulds.—[Mrs. F. H. Thayer.

Frozen Pudding.—Make a good custard, using either whole eggs or the yolks alone. Three yolks or two whole eggs to a pint of milk and one-half cup of sugar. One cup of mixed fruits, one cup of wine, or less wine and one tablespoonful each of brandy and rum. Add cream as you wish and freeze.—[Miss H. L. Day.

Apricot Custard.—One cup of dried apricots, stewed and mashed fine. One-half cup of butter creamed with three-fourths cup of sugar, two eggs, one teaspoonful of cornstarch, one-half cup of sweet milk. Bake in one crust and frost.—[Mrs. P. S. Lehnert.

Apple Compote.—Core, pare and steam eight apples until tender and arrange on an ice-cream platter. Chop some candied pineapple and cherries and cook them in a syrup made with one cup of sugar and one of water. Fill the cores full of the fruit drained from the syrup. Boil the syrup till thick as honey, flavor with lemon juice and pour over the apples. Serve with whipped cream if possible.—[* * * *

Pineapple Pudding.—Quarter of a box of gelatine, half a cup of sugar, and half a pint of boiling water. Soak the gelatine in the juice from the pineapple and add the boiling water and sugar. When cold whip in the well beaten whites of two eggs. Mould and serve with whipped cream.—[Mrs. Charles Knowles.

Bird's Nest Jelly.—Peel and core six apples, put close together in a baking dish and fill the cores with sugar. Bake until they are soft. Soak half a box of gelatine in one cup of water, add two cups of boiling water to dissolve it. Sweeten to taste, add flavoring, wine or lemon juice, and when it begins to thicken pour over the apples. Serve with whipped cream.—[* * * *

ON CAPE COD

Coffee Custard.—One pint of coffee, one cup of cream, heat together and pour onto the yolks of four eggs beaten with one teaspoonful of cornstarch and four tablespoonfuls of sugar. Cook in double boiler until it thickens and the foam is gone. Cool and serve with whipped cream.—[Mrs. E. A. Handy.

Coffee Mousse.—Yolks of four eggs, five ounces of sugar, one cup of strong coffee. Beat the yolks and add the sugar and beat well. Add the coffee hot. When cold add one pint of whipped cream. Pack in salt and ice for four hours.—[Mrs. Charles Knowles.

Savory Apples.—Core apples and set in a pan to bake. Fill holes with mince meat and bake till tender.—[Mrs. E. A. Handy.

Apple Surprise.—Cut apples in halves across the core. Scoop out the core without breaking the skin. Fill the cavities with sugar and a little cinnamon and fasten the halves together with toothpicks. Bake till tender.—[Mrs. E. A. Handy.

Frozen Orange Whip.—Boil together one cup of sugar and two-thirds of a cup of water until thick, add grated rind of two oranges with one-quarter of a cup of orange juice, cover and keep warm one hour, then cool. Beat one pint of cream until stiff and add gradually the orange syrup. Remove the pulp of two oranges, separate into small pieces, drain off the juice, pour it into a mould, then put in alternate layers of whipped cream and orange pulp until mould is full. Pack in salt and ice and let stand two hours (no more). This is delicious.—[Marion M. Copland.

Doughnuts, Cookies and Gingerbread

Molasses Cookies.—One cup of molasses, one cup of butter melted, one-half cup of sugar, one egg dropped in whole and beaten with the other ingredients. One teaspoonful each of soda and ginger, flour to roll out thin.—[Mrs. F. H. Thayer.

Doughnuts.—Butter the size of a walnut creamed with two cups of sugar, three eggs well beaten with the butter and sugar, one cup of milk, one teaspoonful of soda, one teaspoonful of cream of tartar, pinch of salt, nutmeg, five cups of flour, heaping.—[Mrs. F. H. Thayer.

Oat Meal Drop Cakes.—One-half cup of butter creamed with one cup of sugar, two well beaten eggs, one-half cup sour milk, one-quarter teaspoonful of soda, one teaspoonful of cinnamon, one cup of raisins, two cups of flour and two cups of Quaker oats. Drop in cakes and bake thirty minutes. Good.—[Mrs. F. H. Thayer.

Brown Sugar Cookies.—One cup of shortening, two cups of brown sugar, one egg, one-half cup of milk, salt and vanilla, two teaspoonfuls of cream of tartar and one teaspoonful of soda, flour to roll soft. Bake in a quick oven.—[Mrs. Leslie Jones.

ON CAPE COD

Hermits.—Cream together one cup of butter and one and one-half cups of sugar, add two well beaten eggs, one cup of milk, salt, vanilla and one cup of flour which has been sifted with three teaspoonfuls of baking powder, one teaspoonful of cinnamon, one-half teaspoonful of allspice and the same of nutmeg. Add one cup of chopped raisins well floured, one cup of chopped walnuts and flour enough so the dough can be handled. Roll thin and bake in a hot oven.—[Miss Annie Gorham Hinckley.

Good Doughnuts.—Two well beaten eggs, one cup of sugar, one cup of new milk, this will contain about the right amount of shortening; two even teaspoonfuls of cream of tartar, one even teaspoonful of soda, a little salt and nutmeg and flour enough to roll out. Have the fat very hot.—[Mrs. A. G. White.

Brownies.—One cup of sugar, one-half cup of melted butter, two eggs beaten lightly, two squares of chocolate, melted. Flour to make quite stiff, vanilla and nuts. Spread about the thickness of fudge and bake. Cut in squares as soon as taken from the oven. In order to have them moist be careful not to bake too long.—[Miss Annie Gorham Hinckley.

Blitz-kuchen.—One heaping cup of butter creamed with one heaping cup of sugar, add four well beaten eggs and one tablespoonful of vanilla. Sift in two scant cups of flour and one teaspoonful of baking powder. Spread on shallow pan and cover with sugar, cinnamon and blanched almonds. Bake in a moderate oven and cut into squares when done.

Cream Puff Shells.—Two cups of boiling water, two tablespoonfuls of cottolene, a little salt. While boiling add one and a half cups (large) of pastry flour, a little at a time, stir and cook until smooth. When a little cool add four well beaten eggs. Drop on greased tin and bake thirty-five minutes.—[Mrs. Leslie Jones.

Brown Sugar Cookies.—One cup of brown sugar, three-quarters of a cup of melted butter, two well beaten eggs, one teaspoonful of soda, two teaspoonfuls of cream of tartar, one quart of flour and a little vanilla. Very good with chopped peanuts added. A fig filling is also good.—[Miss Annie Gorham Hinckley.

Fairy Gingerbread.—One cup of butter, two cups of sugar, one cup of milk, four cups of flour, three-quarters of a teaspoonful of soda, one tablespoonful of ginger. Beat the butter to a cream, add the sugar gradually, when very light add the ginger, then the milk in which the soda has been dissolved, then the flour. Butter a tin sheet and spread the mixture very thin with a knife. Takes only a short time to bake. When still hot cut into squares.—[Mrs. Peterson.

Doughnuts.—Sift together five cups of pastry flour, one level teaspoonful of soda, two slightly rounding teaspoonfuls of cream of tartar, one teaspoonful of salt, one-half teaspoonful of cinnamon. Beat three eggs very light, add one large cup of sugar and three-quarters of a cup of milk and three tablespoonfuls of thin cream. Roll and cut and let stand on the board one-half hour before frying. They will not soak fat.—[Mrs. E. A. Handy.

ON CAPE COD

GINGERBREAD.—Three-quarters of a cup of molasses, one teaspoonful of soda dissolved in the molasses, one-third of a cup of sugar, one egg, one-half cup of butter, melted. One teaspoonful of ginger, two cups of flour.—[Mrs. F. H. Thayer.

DOUGHNUTS.—One and one-half cups of sugar, saltspoonful of nutmeg, two eggs, beaten together thoroughly. One cup of top milk, flour enough to mix very soft. Mix one heaping teaspoonful of baking powder with the flour. Toss together lightly on the board, roll and cut out as soft as possible to handle.—[Mrs. Alfred Crocker, Jr.

HARD GINGERBREAD.—One-half cup of shortening, one-half cup of sugar, one cup of molasses, two-thirds of a cup of milk, one rounded teaspoonful of soda, ginger and a little salt. Pastry flour to pat out. Bake in moderate oven in a large pan. Cut in squares to take from the pan.—[Mrs. Leslie Jones.

DELICIOUS COOKIES.—One-third of a cup of butter creamed with two-thirds of a cup of sugar, two tablespoonfuls of milk, two cups of flour, two teaspoonfuls of baking powder, one teaspoonful of vanilla and a pinch of salt. Roll very thin and sprinkle with sugar before baking.—[Mrs. Tripp.

SOFT MOLASSES COOKIES.—One cup of sugar, one-half cup of melted lard, two-thirds of a cup of boiling water, two teaspoonfuls of soda, one-half teaspoonful of ginger, one-half teaspoonful of cinnamon, a little salt. Use just enough flour to handle. Do not roll too thin. Bake in a quick oven.—[Mrs. James Holmes.

Soft Molasses Gingerbread.—Two cups of molasses, two-thirds cup of butter, two eggs, one cup of sour milk, one level tablespoonful of soda, same of ginger, a little clove, and one teaspoonful of salt, four cups of pastry flour. Beat the eggs well and add the milk. Heat the molasses and butter together, when hot stir in the soda, spice and salt, as it foams add it to the eggs and milk, beat well and add the flour. Bake in a moderate oven.—[Mrs. E. A. Handy.

Gingerbread Cookies.—Cream one cup of butter, add two cups of sugar and beat well, add two well beaten eggs and half cup of cream, one tablespoonful of ginger and one of cinnamon, one teaspoonful of soda and two of cream of tartar sifted with flour, salt. Flour to roll thin. Cut and sprinkle sugar on top before baking.—[Persis Hayward.

Sugar Cookies.—One cup of butter creamed with two cups of sugar, four eggs beaten separately, one-quarter cup of milk, two teaspoonfuls of baking powder, one teaspoonful of vanilla or a little nutmeg, flour to roll out.—[Mrs. F. H. Thayer.

Swedish Cookies.—One-half cup of butter, one-third cup of sugar, one well beaten egg, three-quarters of a cup of flour, one-half teaspoonful of vanilla. Citron or almonds. Cream the butter, add the sugar gradually, egg, flour and vanilla. Drop in small portions on buttered sheet two inches apart. Spread with a knife dipped in cold water. Put four almonds or four bits of citron on each.—[Mrs. Tripp.

Filled Cookies.—One-half cup of shortening, one cup of sugar, one egg, one-half cup of milk, two teaspoonfuls of cream of tartar, one teaspoonful of soda, one teaspoonful of vanilla, three and a half cups of flour. Filling: One cup of raisins, chopped, one-half cup of sugar, one-half cup of water, one teaspoonful of flour. Cook till thick. Roll dough thin, cut in small rounds, put a little filling on a round and cover with another round, pinch the edges together. Bake in rather a quick oven.—[Mrs. Leslie Jones.

Brownies.—One-third of a cup of butter, one-third of a cup of molasses, one-third of a cup of sugar, one well beaten egg, one cup of flour and one cup of nut meats. Drop by spoonful about an inch apart and bake quickly.—[Mrs. Vaughan Bacon.

Gingerbread.—Three-quarters of a cup of molasses, fill the cup up with sugar, one-half cup of shortening, fill the cup up with hot water, add salt and ginger, three cups of flour and one teaspoonful of soda. Mix well then add one well beaten egg. Bake in a moderate oven.—[Mrs. Leslie Jones.

Cake

In regard to the making of cake, Kate Douglass Wiggin says, "Be sure and have fresh eggs, sweet butter, and good flour and sugar and then remember that all depends upon the woman who puts them together." Aurelia Buck can take good flour and sugar, sweet butter and fresh eggs, and in ten strokes of hand she can make 'em into something the very hogs'll turn away from."—[In "A Village Stradivarius."

COFFEE CAKE.—One cup of butter, one cup of sugar, one cup of molasses, one egg, one cup of cold coffee, one cup of raisins, one cup of chopped walnuts, one tablespoonful of cinnamon, one-half tablespoonful of cloves, one heaping teaspoonful of soda, four and a half cups of flour.—[Miss Annie Gorham Hinckley.

LAZY DAZY CAKE.—Sift together three times, one and one-half cups of flour, one cup of sugar and two teaspoonfuls of baking powder. Put the unbeaten whites of three eggs in a measuring cup and add soft (not melted) butter to half fill the cup, add sweet milk till the cup is full; pour this into the flour mixture and beat seven minutes. This makes a small pan of cake.
—[Mrs. E. A. Handy.

ON CAPE COD

Quick Sponge Cakes.—Separate four eggs, putting the yolks in the mixing bowl and beating till a light yellow. Add gradually one cup of sugar. Beat the whites, adding a pinch of salt, to a stiff froth. Add to the yolks. Sift one teaspoonful of baking powder with one cup of flour and add to the first mixture. Flavor with vanilla or lemon. Pour into muffin pans and bake from twenty minutes to half an hour, according to the heat of the oven. This makes twelve. Very good to take to picnics or to eat with ice cream.—[Mrs. Sprague.

Maple Sugar Frosting.—One cup of maple syrup and a pinch of cream of tartar. Boil till it hairs from the spoon; pour on to the white of one egg beaten stiff. Beat till cool and spread on cake.—[* * * *

Spice Cake.—Three-quarters cup of butter creamed with two cups of sugar, two eggs added whole and beaten well with the butter and sugar, one cup of milk, three cups of flour, one and one-half teaspoonfuls of baking powder, one and one-half cups of raisins, one-half teaspoonful of cinnamon, one-quarter teaspoonful of clove, one-quarter teaspoonful of alspice and a little nutmeg. Sour milk can be used in place of sweet but use soda instead of baking powder.—[Mrs. F. H. Thayer.

Five Egg Sponge Cake.—Yolks of five eggs beaten very light, cut in one cup of sugar, add the juice of one-half of a lemon. Beat the whites of five eggs stiff and cut in slowly, one cup of sifted pastry flour cut in with a knife, one teaspoonful each of vanilla and lemon extract. Bake slowly three-quarters of an hour.—[Miss Elizabeth C. Nye.

GRANDMA HAYWARD'S BLUEBERRY CAKE.—One well beaten egg, add one cup of sugar and one tablespoonful of butter, melted, beat well and add one cup of milk and four cups of pastry flour sifted with three teaspoonfuls of baking powder. Two cups of floured berries. Just before putting in the oven sprinkle with sugar.—[Persis Hayward.

AUNT ANSTIS' CAKE.—Cream one-half cup of butter, add one cup of sugar gradually and beat till creamy. Add four well beaten eggs, one cup of flour and one teaspoonful of baking powder. This calls for an all round flour.—[Mrs. Mary F. Hinckley.

CREAM SPONGE LAYER CAKE.—Beat the yolks of four eggs until thick and lemon colored, add one cup of sugar gradually and beat a couple of minutes then add three tablespoonfuls of cold water. Put one and one-half tablespoonfuls of cornstarch in a cup and fill with flour. Mix and sift flour and cornstarch with one and one-quarter teaspoonfuls of baking powder and one-quarter teaspoonful of salt, add to first mixture. When thoroughly mixed add the whites of four eggs beaten till stiff, and one teaspoonful of lemon extract. Bake thirty minutes in a moderate oven. When cool split cake and spread with currant jelly. Frost with chocolate frosting.—[Mrs. Maurice Hallett.

CHOCOLATE FROSTING.—Whip the whites of two eggs stiff, add confectioner's sugar, two squares of Baker's chocolate and one teaspoonful of butter, melted. Flavor with vanilla.—[Mrs. Maurice Hallett.

LUNCHEON CARAWAY CAKE. — Cream one-quarter of a cup of butter and three-quarters of a cup of sugar, add one well beaten egg. Sift together one tablespoonful of baking powder and one and one-third cups of flour, add this alternately with three-quarters of a cup of milk. One tablespoonful of caraway seeds, three-quarters of a teaspoonful of vanilla and one-quarter of a teaspoonful of salt. Turn in buttered and floured cake pan, sprinkle with sugar and bake. Serve hot.

POTATO CAKE.—One-half cup of butter creamed with two cups of sugar, yolks of five eggs well beaten, one teaspoonful of soda dissolved in one cup of sour milk, one cup of grated chocolate, one-half cup of chopped almonds, one teaspoonful of cinnamon, one-half teaspoonful of allspice, one-quarter of a teaspoonful of cloves, one grated nutmeg, two cups of flour, whites of five eggs, well beaten, one cup of potato well mashed and cold. Mix in the order given and bake in two tins lined with paper.—[Mrs. F. H. Thayer.

HAZELNUT TORTE. German.—Two pounds of nuts weighed in the shell, shell them and grind all but about two dozen. Seven yolks of eggs well beaten, one and one-half cups of sugar, one spoonful of cold water. Beat well, add all but one cup of the grated nuts. One teaspoonful of flour, one teaspoonful of baking powder, whites of four eggs beaten stiff. Bake in two layers. Make a frosting of the three whites of eggs and decorate with the whole nuts candied. Put whipped cream with the remaining grated nuts between the layers. Delicious.—[Mrs. F. H. Thayer.

CHOCOLATE CAKE.—One-half cup of butter creamed with one cup of sugar. Put in a small saucepan four squares of Baker's chocolate, five tablespoonfuls of sugar and two of hot water; melt until smooth and then pour into butter and sugar. Add three well beaten eggs, half a cup of milk, one and three-quarters cups of flour, one-half teaspoonful of soda, and one teaspoonful of cream of tartar. Do not get too stiff. Bake in a moderate oven as the bottom is apt to burn.—[* * * *

POUND CAKE.—Cream one pound of butter, add one pound of sugar and cream together, add ten eggs beaten separately, one pound of flour, one pound of currants, two pounds of raisins, one pound of citron, half a bottle of essence of lemon, half a bottle of essence of vanilla, two tablespoonfuls of all kinds of spices. This will make three large loaves.—[Mrs. F. B. Goss.

WALNUT CREAM PIE.—Three eggs beaten two minutes, add one and one-half cups of sugar and beat five minutes, one-half cup of cold water, two cups of flour and two teaspoonfuls of baking powder, one pound of walnuts, weighed shells and all.—[Mrs. F. H. Thayer.

FROSTING FOR CAKE.—Two cups of sugar, two-thirds of a cup of milk, half of a teaspoonful of butter. Boil five minutes and beat till cool, not cold.—[* * * *

BUTTERCUP CAKE.—One-half cup of butter creamed with one and one-half cups of sugar, yolks of six eggs and one whole egg, one-half cup of milk, two cups of flour, two teaspoonfuls of baking powder, flavoring. Frost with yellow frosting.—[Mrs. F. H. Thayer.

ON CAPE COD

PLUNKETS. Good with ice cream.—Cream one scant cup of butter and one cup of sugar. Beat the yolks and whites of six eggs separately, each until very light then add yolks to whites, fold them together. Add the eggs to the butter and sugar a little at a time. Sift together twice one-half cup of flour, three-quarters cup of cornstarch and two level teaspoonfuls of baking powder, add to the other ingredients and flavor with vanilla. Bake in individual pans. After baking dust with confectioner's sugar. Two scant cups of flour are equal to the cornstarch and flour.—[Mrs. F. H. Thayer.

MRS. MADISON'S OLD-FASHIONED WINE CAKE.—One pound butter, one pound sugar beaten to a cream, add the yolks of six eggs well beaten, one wineglass of brandy, one wineglass of sherry, mace and one whole nutmeg grated, one teaspoonful of soda dissolved in a little hot water, one pound sifted flour, one-half pound currants, washed, dried and floured, one pound raisins chopped, one-half pound citron, sliced thin, cut off all the green rind. Flour all the fruit. Bake in two pans in a moderate oven one and one-quarter hours.—[Grace B. Holway.

MARZIPAN.—Eight eggs, two pounds of flour, two pounds of sugar, one lemon, anise seed. Beat the whites of the eggs to a stiff froth, add the yolks well beaten, sift in the sugar gradually and beat for half an hour, add the grated lemon rind and then the flour, if not firm enough to roll out add more flour, roll rather thin and cut into small cakes, sprinkle with anise seed and stand over night to dry. In the morning bake in a moderate oven.—A German Christmas Cake.

Cape Cod Cake.—One-half cup of butter, one cup of sugar, one egg, one-half cup of molasses, one cup of sour milk, one teaspoonful of soda, five cups of flour, one cup of raisins, spice. —[Miss Annie Gorham Hinckley.

Angel Cake.—One heaping cup of flour measured after sifting, add one teaspoonful of cream of tartar and sift seven times. Beat the whites of eleven eggs very light, add one cup of sugar gradually, one teaspoonful of vanilla and add the flour gradually. Bake one hour.—[Mrs. F. H. Thayer.

Every Day Cake.—Two cups of flour, one cup of sugar, two teaspoonfuls of baking powder sifted together. One-third of a cup of melted butter, add two unbeaten eggs and fill the cup with milk, add this with a little vanilla to the flour mixture and beat well.—[Miss Annie Gorham Hinckley.

Fruit Cake.—Half a pound of butter, half a pound of sugar, five eggs, one-quarter of a teaspoonful of soda dissolved in one-quarter of a cup of molasses, one teaspoonful of all kinds of spices, one-quarter of a bottle of lemon, one-half a tumbler of brandy, three-quarters of a pound of citron, one and a half-pounds of raisins, half a pound of flour. Put fruit in last and bake in a slow oven.—[Mrs. D. M. Seabury.

White Mountain Cake.—One cup of butter creamed with three cups of sugar, one-half cup sweet milk, three and one-half cups of flour sifted with two teaspoonfuls of baking powder, whites of ten eggs. Flavor to taste.—[P. S. Lehnert.

ON CAPE COD

Bridget Powers' Fancy Cake. Old fashioned.—One-half cup of butter, one cup of sugar creamed together, the whites of three eggs beaten stiff, one and one-half cups of sifted flour, one-half small teaspoonful of cream of tartar, one-quarter of a teaspoonful of soda dissolved in one-half cup of milk, almond flavoring. Yellow part: One-half cup of butter, one cup of sugar creamed, one whole egg and the yolks of the three eggs, one-half cup of milk, one-half teaspoonful of cream of tartar, one-quarter of a teaspoonful of soda, one and one-half cups of flour. Flavor with vanilla. Mix the batter in the pans as for marble cake.—[Miss Grace B. Holway.

Shrewsbury Cakes.—One cup of butter creamed with one and one-half cups of sugar, add four well beaten eggs. Beat this mixture until it is light and creamy, then add a little shredded citron and four cups of flour. It should be a thick batter. Drop in small cakes from a spoon on a buttered tin and bake in a good oven. An Old Receipt.

Marlborough Cake.—Four eggs, whites and yolks beaten separately, two cups of sugar, one cup of sweet cream, one-half teaspoonful of soda and one teaspoonful of cream of tartar sifted with two cups of flour.—[Miss Annie Gorham Hinckley.

Marshmallow Frosting.—Boil three-quarters of a cup of sugar and one-quarter of a cup of milk until the syrup threads; do not stir after boiling begins. Cook one-quarter of a pound of marshmallows and two tablespoonfuls of water over boiling water until smooth. Combine the two mixtures and beat until stiff enough to spread. Flavor with vanilla.

Marshmallow Filling.—One-half pound of marshmallows set in the oven until they run together, be careful not to scorch. Boil one cup of sugar with four tablespoonfuls of water until it threads, then pour it over the well beaten white of an egg. Add the melted marshmallows and a little vanilla and beat until stiff enough to spread.

Butter Scotch.—One cup of white sugar, one cup of brown sugar, two tablespoonfuls of vinegar, one-half cup of water and a good piece of butter. Boil until it threads or hardens in cold water.—[Miss Annie Gorham Hinckley.

Angel Cake.—Whites of ten eggs, one and one-half cups of sugar, one teaspoonful of cream of tartar, pinch of salt, one cup of flour, one tablespoonful of water and a little vanilla. Beat the whites of eggs very thoroughly and then beat in the sugar gradually. Sift the flour, salt and cream of tartar together twice and fold lightly into the eggs and sugar. Add vanilla and cold water. Bake in a moderate oven.—[Miss Annie Gorham Hinckley.

Avon Snow Cake.—Cream one cup of butter with two cups of sugar, add one cup of milk, three and a half cups of flour, one-half teaspoonful of soda, one teaspoonful of cream of tartar and the well beaten whites of five eggs. Bake in layers, spread with frosting and grated cocoanut.—[Mrs. D. M. Seabury.

Panuchee.—Two cups of brown sugar, one-half cup of cream, pinch of salt, vanilla, good piece of butter. Chopped nuts, dates, and maraschino cherries. Good with nuts alone.—[Miss Annie Gorham Hinckley.

MARGUERITES.—Two eggs well beaten, one cup of brown sugar, one-third of a teaspoonful of salt, one-quarter of a teaspoonful of baking powder, mix well and one-half cup of flour and one cup of pecan meats. Bake fifteen or twenty minutes in small tins with a nut meat on each one. Bake in a quick oven.—[Mrs. Charles Knowles.

MARGUERITES.—One cup of sugar, one-half cup of water, five marshmallows, the whites of two eggs, two tablespoonfuls of shredded cocoanut, one-half teaspoonful of vanilla, one cup of English walnuts, cut, saltines. Boil the sugar and water till the syrup will thread, remove to back of range and add marshmallows cut in pieces, pour this over the whites of eggs beaten stiff, then add the cocoanut, vanilla and nut meats. Spread the mixture on saltines and bake till delicately brown.—[Mrs. Thomas Lewis.

HOT MILK CAKE.—Two eggs well beaten, one cup of sugar, sift together one cup of flour and one tablespoonful of baking powder twice and add to the eggs and sugar. Scald one-half cup of milk (generous) with a piece of butter the size of a large English walnut and add this hot just before putting in the pan to bake.—[Mrs. Job C. Cobb.

QUICK CAKE.—This is all mixed with an eggbeater in the order given: Two eggs beaten light, one cup sugar, beat well, one tablespoonful melted butter, beat again, one-half cup milk, one and one-half cups flour. Add these, a little of each at a time, and beat till it is full of bubbles. Last of all add one teaspoonful of baking powder. This makes a very light layer cake.—[Mrs. E. A. Handy.

Mocha Tart.—One cup of granulated sugar sifted four times, yolks of four eggs beaten with sugar until light, one and one-half tablespoonfuls of coffee extract, one cup of flour sifted four times with one teaspoonful of baking powder. Beat the whites of five eggs to a froth and add last. Bake in two round tins. Filling: One-half pint of cream whipped, sugar to taste, one and one-half tablespoonfuls of coffee extract. Icing: One and one-half tablespoonfuls of coffee extract stirred well with one cup of confectioner's sugar. Add one teaspoonful of cold water at a time until thin enough to spread.—[Miss Elizabeth C. Nye.

Delicate Cake.—One-half cup of butter creamed with one and one-half cups of sugar, one-half cup of milk, two and one-half cups of flour, two teaspoonfuls of baking powder, whites of five eggs beaten stiff.—[Mrs. F. H. Thayer.

Spanish Bun.—Cream one cup of butter with two cups of light brown sugar, add the yolks of two eggs and two whole ones well beaten. One small teaspoonful of cinnamon and the same of cloves, one cup of milk and two of flour, two teaspoonfuls of baking powder. Bake in a good sized dripping pan; when cool turn out and cut in squares. Make a boiled frosting using the two whites of eggs and frost the top and sides of each square. —[* * * *

Delicate Cake.—Cream one cup of butter with two cups of sugar. Sift three cups of flour, four tablespoonfuls of cornstarch and three teaspoonfuls of baking powder together and add alternately with one cup of milk. Last of all add the whites of four eggs beaten to a stiff froth.—[* * * *

MOTHER'S SPONGE CAKE.—Six eggs, one and one-half cups of sugar, one and one-half cups of flour, juice and grated rind of one lemon, half a teaspoonful of salt. Separate the yolks and whites of the eggs; add the lemon to the yolks and beat, add half the sugar and beat again, add the remaining sugar and beat light. Beat the whites and the salt to a dry froth and add to the yolks and sugar and beat hard for five minutes or until the bubbles rise and break. Cut the flour in lightly. Bake in a slow oven about an hour.—[Mrs. E. A. Handy.

WEDDING CAKE.—One and one-half cups of butter creamed with one and one-half cups of sugar, one cup of molasses, four eggs, one teaspoonful of soda in four and one-half cups of flour. One pound raisins, one pound currants, one-half pound citron, one teaspoonful of cloves, cinnamon, and nutmeg. Mix and let it stand over night. Bake four hours.—[P. S. Lehnert.

Pastry

Sour Milk Pie.—One cup of sour milk, one cup of chopped raisins, one teaspoonful each of cloves, cinnamon and nutmeg, a little salt, two eggs and one cup of sugar. This makes two pies. —[Mrs. A. G. White.

Lemon Pie.—Beat to a froth one and one-half cups of sugar, the rind and juice of one and one-half lemons and the yolks of three eggs. Then beat the whites of three eggs and stir in with one and one-half tablespoons of milk. Turn into a plate already prepared and bake in a moderate oven forty-five minutes.—[Josephine Farrington.

Chocolate Pie.—Two cups of milk, four eggs, four tablespoonfuls of sugar, two and one-half tablespoonfuls of grated chocolate, pinch of salt and a little vanilla. Melt chocolate and stir in a little milk and when well mixed add the rest of the milk with the yolks of three eggs and one whole egg well beaten, sugar, salt and vanilla. Stir well and bake in a plate lined with pie crust. Have the oven moderate and be careful not to burn. Cool and frost with the whites of three eggs and three teaspoonfuls of sugar.—[Mrs. Mary Freeman Hinckley.

ON CAPE COD

Delicious Filling for Turnovers.—Mix well one egg, one cup of sugar, juice and grated rind of one lemon, one tablespoon cornstarch, two tablespoons milk, one-half tablespoon butter and one cup boiling water. Cook till thick and add one-half cup of seeded raisins. When cold use for turnovers or for filling for pie with two crusts.—[Mrs. E. A. Handy.

Apple Pot Pie.—Peel and quarter apples. Stew with a little water and when soft add sugar and cinnamon to taste. Make dumplings of one cup pastry flour, one rounding teaspoon baking powder and one-quarter teaspoon salt. Mix with milk just stiff enough to roll out. Cut in rounds and drop in the boiling apple sauce. Cover tight and keep boiling for ten or more minutes. Try with a straw and serve as soon as cooked or they will be soggy. These dumplings can be dropped from a spoon into the hot apple sauce to save time.—[Mrs. E. A. Handy.

Delaps.—Four apples, remove skins and cores, put through a meat chopper or chop in bowl. Measure and add an equal amount of sugar and the grated rind and juice of a lemon. Line patty pans with pie paste and fill with the mixture. Bake in a moderate oven until the apple is red. Serve with whipped cream Variations: Bake in pie plate and cover with meringue as for lemon pie. If apples are not acid use less sugar.—[Mrs. E. A. Handy.

Wholesome Apple Pie.—Slice apples thin to fill a pie plate heaping full. Add one cup sugar and half a level teaspoon each of cinnamon and nutmeg. Cover with a good pie paste and bake one hour in a moderate oven. Just before putting in the oven dash some cold water over the crust. It will make it flaky and crisp.—[Mrs. E. A. Handy.

ECCLES.—One large cup of seeded and chopped raisins, one cup of sugar, one teaspoonful of cinnamon, one-quarter teaspoonful of nutmeg, and the same of cloves, two tablespoonfuls of strong coffee and one tablespoonful of brandy or rum. Make a rich piecrust. Roll and cut with medium sized cookie cutter, two rounds for each eccle. Put one teaspoonful of the mixture on the bottom round, wet the edge as for a pie, gash the top round and put in place, pressing together around the edge with a fork dipped in flour. The filling will make three dozen "Eccles."—[Mrs. Alfred Crocker, Jr.

Pickles and Preserves

CLUB SAUCE.—Six large tomatoes, one green pepper, (without the seeds), one onion, one cup of sugar, two cups of vinegar and two tablespoonfuls of salt. Chop all fine and boil to the consistency of catsup.—[Mrs. Leslie Jones.

SPICED APPLE JELLY.—One-half peck of apples, one pint of vinegar, three pints of water, one ounce of stick cinnamon, one-half ounce of whole cloves. Cook the apples with the vinegar and water and spices. Strain and use a pint of fruit juice to a pint of sugar as in any jelly.—[Mrs. Peterson.

CRANBERRY SAUCE.—Boil one quart of water and three cups of sugar ten minutes, add three pints of cranberries and let it boil up once. Cover and set on the back of the stove to simmer but not boil, twenty minutes. Cool and serve the next day when it is at its best.—[Mrs. B. D. Peterson, Jr.

SPICED CURRANTS.—Seven pounds of currants, five pounds of brown sugar, three tablespoonfuls of cinnamon, three tablespoonfuls of cloves, one pint of vinegar. Wash the currants and remove the stems; put in kettle with the sugar and vinegar, add the spices tied in a muslin bag. Cook slowly an hour and a half. —[Mrs. Peterson.

Spice Jelly.—One peck of apples, five cups of vinegar, three cups of water, half ounce of whole cloves, half ounce of allspice, one ounce of cinnamon bark. Cut apples, without paring or coring; put in kettle with spices, vinegar and water and boil until soft. Suspend the compound in a bag to extract the juice. Measure the juice and allow one pound of sugar to each pint. Put the juice back on the fire and heat the sugar in the oven. When the juice boils add the sugar and simmer three-quarters of an hour.—[Mrs. H. M. Hutchings.

Spiced Grapes.—Eight pounds of grapes and eight pounds of sugar, one pint of vinegar, one tablespoonful each of cloves, cinnamon, allspice and mace. Press the pulp of the grapes from the skins one at a time, boil the pulp a few minutes and strain out the seeds. Add the skins and boil slowly half an hour, add the other ingredients and boil till thick. Be careful it does not burn.—[Mrs. E. A. Handy.

Pear Relish.—Three-fourths of a pound of sugar to each pound of pear sliced thin. Let stand over night, in the morning add one-quarter pound of ginger root tied in a thin cloth. Cook several hours.—[Mrs. F. H. Thayer.

Grape Fruit Marmalade.—One grape fruit, one orange, one lemon. Three quarts of cold water, three quarts of sugar. Peel and cut the rind in slivers with scissors. Put the pulp through a meat chopper, add three quarts of water, let it stand over night, the next day boil half an hour, let stand twenty-four hours, boil one hour and add three quarts of sugar, boil till it jellies. This makes eight glasses.—[Mrs. E. A. Handy.

ON CAPE COD

TOMATO MARMALADE.—Four pounds of ripe tomatoes, peeled, four pounds of sugar, six lemons and one cup of raisins. Remove the seeds from raisins and lemons and chop with tomatoes. Add the sugar and boil slowly together two hours. Put hot into glass.—[Mrs. Howard.

SUGARED GRAPE FRUIT RIND.—Cut rind in strips and soak forty-eight hours in salt and water, one tablespoonful of salt to one quart of water. Drain and cook eight hours in fresh water, changing water two or three times. Cook one hour in a syrup made of one pound of sugar to one-half cup of water for each pound of rind. Boil until the syrup is nearly boiled away. Drain, cool and roll in powdered sugar.—[Mrs. Ruth E. Chipman.

QUINCE HONEY.—To one large quince grated, add one cup of sugar and a little water. Boil till clear.—[* * * *

ORANGE MARMALADE. A Cuban Receipt.—Messina or Valencia oranges. Peel off the yellow rind very thin, soak twenty-four hours in salt and water. Next day boil the peels three hours in fresh water, changing the water two or three times. Peel off all the white skin on the oranges and throw it away. Cut up the fruit in very small pieces, taking out all the seeds. Cut the yellow peel in narrow strips. Weigh peel, oranges and juice, and to every pound or pint add a little less than a pound of granulated sugar. Boil until thick and clear; from an hour to an hour and a half. Some prefer three-quarters of a pound of sugar to a pound of fruit.—[Miss H. L. Day.

Sweet Corn Pickle.—One dozen ears corn cut from the cob, one large head of cabbage, chopped, six green peppers, chopped, eight onions, chopped, three stalks of celery, chopped, three cups of brown sugar, three small tablespoons salt, three pints vinegar, four tablespoons dry mustard, one tablespoon tumeric, two tablespoons celery seed. Boil forty-five minutes and can.—[Mrs. E. A. Handy.

Sliced Pickles.—Pare and slice very thin one dozen cucumbers. Sprinkle with salt and let stand three or four hours, then drain. Take one quart of cold vinegar, half a cup each of black and white mustard seed, six onions cut small, three-quarters of a cup of salad oil and one tablespoonful of celery seed. Mix all well together and pour over the cucumbers.—[Mrs. Walter Tufts.

Uncooked Chili Sauce.—One peck of ripe tomatoes, cut fine, sprinkle with one cup of salt and drain, eight stalks of celery cut in small pieces, four green peppers chopped, do not use seeds, one cup of chopped onion, one cup of horse radish, one cup of mustard seed, two cups of sugar, two teaspoonfuls of black pepper, same of cloves and cinnamon, one quart of vinegar. Mix well and seal in jars.—[Mrs. E. A. Handy.

Lemon Marmalade.—One lemon, one cup of water, one cup of sugar. Peel the yellow rind from the lemon and cut it in thin strips, boil it in a pint of water for one hour, drain and throw away the water. Chop the lemon pulp, free it from seeds, add one cup of water and the rind, boil one hour, add the sugar and boil about fifteen minutes, or until it jellies.—[Mrs. E. A. Handy.

ON CAPE COD

CHOW CHOW.—One large cauliflower and two quarts of small string beans broken in pieces and parboiled. One quart of onions, peeled, one quart of ripe cucumbers peeled and cut in inch pieces, one quart of small cucumbers, one quart of green tomatoes, add six green peppers cut small, do not use the seeds of the peppers. Stand in weak brine for twenty-four hours, scald in the same brine, drain and while still hot pour over the following mixture: One cup of flour, six tablespoonfuls of dry mustard, one tablespoonful of tumeric, one and one-half cups of brown sugar sifted together and mixed to a paste with a little cold vinegar, stir this carefully into two quarts of hot cider vinegar, cook slowly until it thickens, stirring all the time, seal in jars while hot.—[* * * *

Miscellaneous

"Now may good digestion wait on appetite,
And health on both!"
—[Shakespeare.

CREAM SAUCE.—One tablespoonful of butter, one tablespoonful of flour, one cup of milk. Melt the butter, add the flour and stir till smooth, add the milk slightly warm and cook till thick, stirring all the time. This will never be lumpy.—[Mrs. E. A. Handy.

STUFFED PRUNES.—Four dozen prunes boiled until tender in unsweetened water. Drain until thoroughly dry and remove the stones. Make a paste of cream cheese with chopped walnuts for filling. Serve with salad.—[Miss Marvin.

*CHILE CON CARNE. Mexican receipt. — One and one-half pounds tender raw beef, one onion, one-half can tomatoes, one-half pod red pepper. Hash the beef fine; put it to cook with sufficient cold water; with this mix the chopped onion and pepper. Stew until well done and almost dry. Then add tomato and scald.—[Miss D. E. Hinckley.

*From Midsummer Cook Book.

ON CAPE COD

"They have in Turkey a drink called Coffee. This drink comforteth the brain and heart and helpeth the digestion."—[Bacon.

Boiled Coffee.—The coffee must be freshly ground, failing that warm it in the oven stirring often, be careful it does not brown any more than when you put it in. For six cups take six tablespoonfuls of coffee, one yolk of egg and cold water enough to make a thin paste. Let this stand for five minutes or an hour if more convenient, add six cups of cold water. Put over a hot fire and the minute it begins to boil stir it down and then let it boil up once more. Set it where it will keep hot but not boil, until it settles.—[Mrs. E. A. Handy.

Chocolate Fudge.—One quart of sugar, one-quarter of a pound of Baker's chocolate, one-half cup of milk, butter the size of an egg. Cook till it hardens in water, flavor and beat a few minutes.—[Mrs. Lottie C. Holmes.

Sea Foam.—Three cups of brown sugar, one cup of water, one tablespoonful of vinegar. Boil until it threads. Then beat into it the whites of two eggs which have been beaten light, add vanilla and nuts. Beat fifteen minutes or so and drop on buttered paper. —[Miss Annie Gorham Hinckley.

Baked Beans.—Soak one quart of beans over night, in the morning rinse well. Put in the bean pot with three-quarters of a pound of pork, one tablespoonful of molasses and one teaspoonful of salt. Bake all day.—[Mrs. Job C. Cobb

D. A. R. Punch.—One dozen oranges, one dozen lemons, one can of grated pineapple, one quart bottle of raspberry juice, one glass of grape jelly, six cups of sugar, one quart of water, one quart of apollinaris added at intervals while being served. Sufficient for fifty people.—[Miss Marvin.

In the name of the Village Improvement Society I wish to thank all those Cape Cod housekeepers who have so kindly contributed their favorite receipts and so made this book of real use as well as of interest.

We are indebted to Miss Irene Loring for the design for the cover.

AMY L. HANDY, Compiler.

K